REVIEWS

This book is highly educative and contains the basic practical principles of achieving a successful relationship in your marriage. This is a highly recommended book for every religious leader as a teaching tool in their various churches or organisations as well as couples who aim at achieving tremendous success and progress in their relationships.

Dossah Mawunyega (Evangelist)

From this book, the author highlighted the need to be aware of certain pitfalls that can hinder the success of relationships. Pitfalls, dangers, risks or difficulties are inherent in relationships for you are different people, from different backgrounds, experience and probably culture etc....It does not matter who you used to be, what matters is who you choose and decide to be for you are offered a new opportunity with each breathe to think, choose, decide and act differently in a way that supports and builds your relationship. Regret is hard to live with especially when you know you could avoid the mistakes.

Oluwa Tosin Inestimable Grace. (Marketing Director)

I thank God that this book is coming out at a time that there is great concern for the deteriorating life in the marriage home. Arguably, the reason why so many homes are collapsing is because they lack this important information about the institution of marriage. As is it common in life, whatever you go into without enough information or knowledge, you are bound to fail. This book, therefore, will certainly be of a blessing to young and old couples and even to those who are yet to marry.

Rev. Dr. Ray Edem St. James (Apostle) Triumphant Christian Global Mission (UK)

Relationship without serious communication will always be opened to disaster and disappointments. When this happens, the relationship becomes vulnerable and attacked by negative friends whose intention is to ruin it. Many lessons to be learnt from this great book.

Apostle Emmanuel Mensah (Ghana)

The author wrote this with complete respect and passion for one another's feelings. He broke it all down in an understanding way that helps guide partners stopping relationship breakdowns. Household chores can cause so much heartache and every word the author wrote will help save a relationship. Extremely informative read.

Dr Karen Johnson (Author, Out of the Corner) United Kingdom

6. Mr. Ferdinard Senyo Lawson is a very relational person and full of practical wisdom that he fully accredits to the grace of God upon His life. I had a lot of aha moments when I read this life changing book. I will highly recommend this book to couples and aspiring couples. This is a precious book and a gift to the body of Christ.

Joana Okudzeto Biekro (A Christian Counsellor)

This book carries every tool that is needed to fix a home that is facing diversities of trials. It is also a book that will empower and enrich couples. It is very informative and impactful. It is a book that will help to redirect your mind on how to handle your spouse so that you can both have a marital bliss. We have read it ourselves and strongly recommend it to all married and every child of God intending to go into relationship. Knowledge is power. GET THIS BOOK..

Rev. Ola & Rev. (Mrs) Stella David.
(To Nourish & To Cherish Marriage Ministries)

People are lonely because they build walls instead of bridges. Ferdinard Senyo Lawson endeavors to show married couples how to prevent the construction of walls between one another. This is very important since the Apostle Peter declares that the lack of honor between a husband and his wife can actually hinder their prayers! (I Peter 3:7)

God designed marriage to produce "a godly seed" (Malachi 2:15). Christianity is only one generation away from extinction. The greatest lessons in life are caught, not taught. When children see God's love consistently modeled before them by their parents, they can readily recognize the inherent value and lasting benefits of being faithful to the Lord throughout their lives.

Marriage puts people into a most vulnerable situation in which one can be easily hurt.However, marriage should be the safest place on earth. It can be that, by the help of the Lord, when the husband and wife each place the needs of the other above one's own (Philippians 2:3-4).

Marriage is not two people coming together to live for each other. Instead, it is two people coming together to live for the Lord. Such a couple can, thereby, accomplish more together than they ever could have done before. It is glorious when a married couple lives in heavenly harmony -- serving the Lord as a team. God is honoured, and His work is promoted. The world certainly needs to see more of that.

It is our prayer that this book will greatly assist married couples in achieving that worthy goal.

Pastor Edward E. Young,
Jackson, Michigan

LET'S TALK ABOUT IT *Baby*

—————— VOLUME 1 ——————

FERDINARD SENYO LAWSON
Multiple Award-Winning Best Author
BA. (HONS) IN PUBLIC HEALTH & SOCIAL CARE

FOREWORD BY
REV.DR. FRIMPONG YAW MANSO

© 2016

First published in Ghana by;
Hetura Books Co. Ltd
Location: Tema, Ghana
Publishing | Events | Consulting
Mobile: +233-307-001-724 | +233-244-962-930

Hetura

DEDICATION

This book is affectionately dedicated to my deceased grandmother, **Madam Felicia Ami Ocloo,** who never gave up on me but dedicated her lifetime to introduce me to my Maker (GOD). Grandma, thank you and may your soul continue to rest with God. Introducing me to Jesus Christ was the best gift you have left with me.

My wife, Deborah, and my children, Joshua and Jessica, words cannot express how much I love you. You have inspired me to write this book. I dedicate the book to you as well.

ACKNOWLEDGEMENT

First and foremost I would like to thank the Trinity (God, Jesus Christ, and the Holy Ghost) for the grace to write this book. I want to thank God for keeping my wife and me for twelve years in marriage this year (2016). It has never been easy for the past twelve years in marriage but the grace and mercy of God have made it possible for us to stay in marriage. We have thus become a testimony to many young marriages. Thank you Lord as we step forward into the next phase of our marriage.

To my beloved pastor and a friend, **APOSTLE LAWERENCE ACHIAPONG,** whose prayer and support never ceases. Not forgetting the entire membership of THE WORD OF GOD MINISTRY- LONDON for your kindness and love towards my family. May God bless you all.

To Rev. Dr Paul Yaw Frimpong-Manso *(General Superintendent of the General Council of Assemblies of God, Ghana)*, words cannot express my gratitude to the committee for your support, kindness, prayer and encouragement. You dedicated your time in writing the foreword for this book simply because you believed in the information and the revelations in it. Few words are only used to describe great men like you. Thank you for the seed you have sown in my life. God bless you.

My sincere gratitude goes to my spiritual mentor, Pastor Charles Owusu *(Deeper Christian Life Bible Church. Ghana)*, who I first served faithfully and in loyalty an Armor Bearer back in my youthful days in Ghana for many years. You are a great inspiration to me and my family both here in United Kingdom and Ghana. God bless you.

To my spiritual mentor, **Rev. Kingsley Amoah of Everlasting Life Ministry**; words will not be enough for me to express my sincere gratitude and appreciation to you. You have been a strong pillar of encouragement and inspiration to me and most importantly, my family. God bless you.

To **Bishop Dr. Julius K Owusu-Ansah,** words cannot express my gratitude to the committee for your support, kindness, prayer and encouragement. God bless you.

To my parents, **MR and MRS Lawson,** and my siblings, God bless you so much for the foundation of education and training you gave me during my formative years. May God continue to keep you alive to reap the fruits of your hard work. Your labour shall not be in vain.

To my parents-in-law, especially His **Excellency Mr. Justice Joseph B. Akamba;** you instilled in me the idea to turn my knowledge into articles. I can gratefully say that they are now in books. I want to say thank you so much for being an inspiration. God bless you.

I would like to thank a few of people who helped to review this book. I am genuinely humbled by your time and sacrifice spent to bring this book into reality. Only God can reward you all.

I would also like to express my gratitude to the entire team at Hetura Books (Ghana) for editing/proof reading, designing the cover, and the interior decoration of the book. God richly bless you.

TABLE OF CONTENTS

FOREWORD

Let's Talk About It Baby is a priceless, down-to-earth piece about challenges in relationships. It is short, crisp and easy to read. The book establishes the importance of COMMUNICATION in any relationship especially marital. It has a lot of real and practical descriptions of challenges of relationships which all who seek good and successful relationships need to pay attention to.

Interesting ideas are presented in a simple and warm manner such that the reader feels the presence of the author as in a chat room communicating. I recommend this book for both practice and research since it has a great store of practical and in-depth knowledge and would heal any aching relationship with the help of the Almighty. Let's talk about the real issues for there is no love without communication…

Rev. Dr. Paul Frimpong Manso
General Superintendent of Assemblies of God
Ghana

INTRODUCTION

"Everybody has the need to be listened to and be fully understood."

It takes two people to have an effective and productive conversation at any level. This implies that for people or couples to have a solid relationship, they must ensure that communication is put in the heart of that relationship to start with. Two people cannot walk together except they agree and the only thing that makes that possible is effective communication.

Couples should be able to feel free to talk about things without their partner feeling undermined, disregarded or disrespected on a view that may be sensitive to him or her.

Observably, one of the main reasons why relationships don't work effectively is because people are not talking or are refusing to communicate as they should. Hence, this causes each other pain and frustration within the relationship.

It is true that people are different on the basis of their backgrounds, values, outlooks or views (perceptions) which create different comfort zones for them. So, talking about issues or challenges within the relationship is seen as a hurdle. This then discourages them from talking about serious issues within their relationship because they do not want to be seen by their partners as nagging or causing trouble.

When people fail to talk about issues within their relationships, it creates unnecessary misunderstanding, distance, indifference

1

and even competition, aggression and verbal violence towards each other simply because issues have not been discussed.

Relationship is the centre of our lives and it takes communication to express the love we have for each other. When this is achieved, it can easily lead to feelings of joy for being together, light-heartedness, inner peace, contentment with life, a deep inner wisdom with each other.

Therefore, this book is written to help rebuild relationships that are on the verge of break-up. It serves as a fence-builder to prevent other relationships from falling into the ditch of separation especially when the partners pay attention to effective communication.

Although it is a fact that some people find it difficult to talk about some vital personal experiences especially subjects like their childhood relationships and how it ended up badly, or their past life due to negative flashbacks or hurts, it is my heart's desire that after reading this book, partners will relearn and learn how to talk to each other more regardless of the challenging issues.

This will develop love and affection for each other as they embrace their various differences; communicate more effectively and openly without fear but in respect to avoid unnecessary misunderstandings that have plagued many relationships causing hurt, anger, confusion and painful divorce over the years.

"LET'S TALK ABOUT IT BABY"
IS THE BOOK FOR YOUR RELATIONSHIP'S
REVIVAL

Chapter One

THE VALUE OF COMMUNICATION IN YOUR RELATIONSHIP

E verything about a relationship is built around communication. It plays a vital role in sustaining or breaking the relationship. The lack of communication in any relationship whatsoever will lead to its failure. Communication is everything in life. Life cannot be interesting without communication. In fact, without effective communication, life is meaningless.

Communication helps us give and receive information from our partner. As couples, we communicate with each other not only face to face, but also through body language, writings and symbols.

Just as oxygen is to the body, communication is also vital in determining the quality of relationship we have with each other especially in business and family.

3

Communication is the foundation

This therefore means that communication plays a major role in bonding couples. This can be in the form of nonverbal and verbal depending on the type of relationship one has with their partner. Our body movements, gestures, facial expressions, and hand movements all communicate something to our partners.

When we engage in communication with our partners, we are able to express our ideas and feelings and it helps us to understand the emotions and thoughts of the other partner. When communication goes wrong, partners develop the wrong feelings towards each other and even other people. It is no doubt that communication plays a vital role in building the relationships of couples.

This however indicates that each partner or party must learn to cultivate the habit of communicating effectively to their partners so as to see their relationship blossom like a watered garden.

Communication is like a vital organ system (the heart) that allows the free movement of ideas, thoughts, dreams, and emotional feelings to be aired to strengthen the relationship.

When you observe the heart organ, it is responsible for the blood flow to the whole body. Therefore, when the heart fails, the body dies because there wouldn't be blood flow (oxygen) to the other parts of the body. It is possible therefore to say that communication is the heart organ of every relationship; which means that, when communication fails, everything within it also dies.

Communication can be seen as manure or fertilizer enhancing the strength and providing nutrients to our relationships. This allows our relationship as plants to grow. When communication is missing in any kind of relationship, the relationship suffers from nutrient deficiency and stops growing.

When couples fail to talk about things within their relationships, it prevents vital and valuable things to be discussed and shared to demonstrate love and care to each other.

Couples should be ready and prepared to invest into their relationships through effective communication. They should never avoid talking about issues for fear of their partner's reaction. This is because for our relationships to function and thrive properly, things must be talked about and aired effectively until all the issues at hand are resolved.

Mistakes are everywhere and our relationships are not different but the attitude or approach towards it is what determines how we overcome the mistakes and hurdles of communication. No matter how well we think of our partners, we should spend time to talk about things to avoid misunderstandings in our relationships.

Most people use nonverbal form of communication in their relationships, however. It is the best form of talking and resolving issues within the relationship. Every relationship is different from others and it is vital that each couple discovers and identifies the best form of communication for them in discussing and sharing ideas.

Although nonverbal communication plays a major role in relationships by helping to convey meaning in different ways, it is important for couples to choose their words carefully to help communicate effectively.

It is much better and easier to identify any shortcomings which can be improved on when couples learn to talk about things most often. For couples who are serious about the longevity of their relationship and to limit or reduce unnecessary misunderstandings, it is crucial to lay more emphasis on talking about things within the relationship openly and honestly.

When things are talked about in a relationship, it helps to diffuse any form of anger, removes guilt and builds stronger and better union within the relationship. Each partner gets a fair deal from the relationship especially when they communicate effectively in ways that both understand. This enables them to help each other achieve a common goal.

Without effective communication, nothing can be achieved. It is evident that trust and confidence can be built in a relationship where communication is seen as a priority. Partners have stronger understanding and confidence in each other and are able to share thoughts and emotions in ways that encourage both party to support and help if need be.

You can't be in any relationship and be selfish. Communication in a relationship should never be a one-way traffic but a two-way. Talking about issues should not be what one partner wants without thinking about his or her partner's feelings. Therefore, when people express their thoughts and ideas comfortably, it helps to discover what each partner wants without feeling being talked at or controlled.

Talking about things helps to bring about transparency into relationships and creates the platforms on which issues are tackled in love and with respect. It has the potential to remove any form of doubt and insecurity, loss of hope, and emotional

> ❝
> **"A healthy relationship is only possible if you sit and talk about things."**
> **FERDINARD SENYO LAWSON**

breakdown which sometimes affect and destroy the relationship.

Two people living together in a relationship is fun only when both parties are ready to talk about things in a sensible and mature manner without one party feeling deprived or deceived. Openness is one of the benefits of effective communication within a relationship. It helps partners to understand and adapt to each other's flaws and mistakes. The only way to understand someone is to learn to talk to them. This is the more reason why people are encouraged to talk about things in any relationship.

Over the years since married to my wife, I have personally observed that our trust for each other builds up stronger when we let things out by talking about them. We are not perfect but talking about issues that bother us individually help us to realign ourselves and build the confidence and trust we had for each when we first met.

There are difficult times in every relationship but with effective communication, those hurdles or challenges are levelled and love is ignited. My wife and I have discovered that in order for us to have a healthy relationship and live longer to achieve our dreams and aspirations and to help our children appreciate and learn how to talk to us, it is important that we create time to speak to each other as often as we can.

Often, I have the desire to travel for mission work and my wife will not be in agreement simply because I have not been able to communicate the vision and the purpose for that mission. This therefore creates insecurity and lack of support on her part. When this happens, I cancel the mission trip to avoid unnecessary misunderstanding and problems arising which may have the potential to affect me more than her.

If you ever wanted a support from your partner, then you must learn to talk about things. Talk openly to your partner and create the right environment where you can both share ideas and feelings. Again, I have discovered that we get closer to each other when we talk openly on matters that are beyond us.

Talking to each other about anything helps us to know how much we need each other to achieve success within the family union. We are ready and able to support any idea raised by each of us and have each other's backing. This is what a healthy relationship is about.

No love without communication

Love is actually built on the platform of communication. So when this fails, love is broken allowing all sorts of negative things to slip through to break the relationship. Doubt, misunderstandings, insecurities, mistrust or faithlessness are some of the other negative things that can be created if things are not talked about within the relationship.

It is advisable that couples learn to understand the need to talk about things to each other if only they want to save their relationship. It takes a lot to build a healthy relationship so never allow silence treatment destroy or kill your relationships. Whatever the issue seems to be, it is time to talk about it.

It is very necessary for each partner to come out clearly with what they want to talk about. This is how relationships grow and yield much fruits. We may not always be in the position to agree with our partners but talking about things put the relationship on a solid ground to provide emotional support, help in making decisions, and encouragement concerning the future.

Set aside quality time

In order to get the best out of any communication within the relationship, partners should be able to set aside suitable time for both of them to talk about things without being interrupted or disturbed by their children or phone calls.

It is also useful to change location or environment to talk about things. Nothing should be left hanging or unaddressed in the relationship. A good environment can be created to talk which may include taking a walk, a visit to the beach or a place that brings good memories to both partners. That period can be used to express how you feel about each other and try to resolve any ill feelings that could disable the relationship. This is the time to talk about things.

Chapter Two

TALK ABOUT YOUR FINANCIAL ISSUES
(MONEY MATTERS)

Never Ever Let Financial Issues Destroy Your Relationship

Money has always been a form of defence to every relationship. Any country without a defending system is bound to be overthrown or overcome by enemies. In a similar context, a relationship cannot stand or last without money. Money plays a vital role in binding and solidifying relationships and everything around us is centred on money. This is the more reason why every partner needs to talk about money in their relationships.

Talks about sex should not be more than financial management in a relationship. You will be amazed to discover the number of relationships that have broken down because of money.

Today, it is possible to say that financial freedom has become a tool in bringing peace and longevity in most relationships and providing couples freedom to pursue their dreams.

Therefore, it is important to know that as much as money is good in binding couples, we need to accept that it may not necessarily buy anyone happiness if truth is not attached to money. Couples need to make time to talk about their financial matters. This helps couples to establish a good relationship with money and how they can tackle any issue that may arise in the relationship due to lack of understanding.

Everybody is different and with different spending habits. Thus, living together as couples in a relationship, you must be opened to talk about money if only you both want to have a future together. Spend quality time to discover the kind of attitude your partner has regarding money. Just like anything else, discovering your attitude to money gives you the platform to have a better understanding of how both of you spend money.

Some couples are very good at managing money. Each partner knows the type of person they are dealing with when it comes to money management in the relationship. Some are able to identify themselves as spenders, misers, wasters, and money-haters. Depending on whatever each partner's strengths or weaknesses are, find time to talk about money as it helps to know how to deal with money matters when the heat is on.

As a lifestyle coach, I have witnessed instances where money has played a major part in relationship breakdown. Happy and lovely marriages have ended up in terrible divorce simply because money has been given the power to destroy the relationship. Money matters have caused more arguments in most relationships than anything else because of different perspective about how to handle finances.

Don't let money matters control your relationship

You will be very surprised to find out the number of divorces that occur as a result of money matters. Money is a powerful energy that drives and controls relationships and if time is not allocated to talk about it, it destroys the relationship. Whatever thought each partner has, it is necessary to talk about it and be clear on how partners in the relationship want to handle their financial issues. This helps to create an atmosphere of peace and love.

Relationships are great treasures to have but when things are not dealt with sensibly through effective communication, lives are damaged or disabled.

It is better to talk about things and find solutions to problems than to assume and let money dig a hole in your relationship beyond repair. It is good to talk about matters bordering on money. You must both decide as couples when it is appropriate to sit down and discuss how money is being spent in the relationship. This must be done in a mutual and respectful manner.

Never talk about money when one partner is busy or distracted by a football game or breakfast. Time must be allocated for sensitive matters in order to gain full results.

Money can cause friction in any relationship. Talk about it regardless

Years back, my wife and I had argued over money and how it should be spent. This brought a lot of headache to us especially me as I love to be very calculative and see myself as a wise spender whiles Deborah loves to spend money on any need that arises. We spent hours and hours arguing about what the money was spent on in a very bad and terrible manner.

This did not help the two of us and it was very important for both of us to agree and make peace so that the children would not be affected negatively.

Money can be a good servant but a terrible master

My wife and I have come a long way with how we handle our discussion about money as we grow together by the grace of God. We are now wiser in how we handle our finances. I have devised a monthly expenditure plan to help us organise our financial commitments. This has been helpful for us.

Never see argument over money as the licence to separate or divorce your partner. It takes time to come to the full understanding of each other's spending habits. Remember that there is no relationship without argument. Thus, learn to talk about things and find solutions to them. Your relationship is very different from your next door neighbour's. So you must always learn to talk about money matters the best way that fits your relationship.

Talk about money matters in your relationships before things get out of hands

Whatever the case may be, never leave your money matters unattended to. One of you must take the bull by the horns and tackle the issues around your finances to avoid their turning into insurmountable obstacles. Create time for both of you to talk about your financial issues in a relaxed mood.

Talking about money in a relationship must not end up in an argument or fight. So, it is advisable not to talk about money matters when one party is angry. Nobody makes sense when they are angry. Talking about money matters in an angry mood will only aggravate and escalate issues like adding more petrol to fire. Create time and space for it.

Avoid talking about money issues when your partner is angry

Not everyone likes to talk about money. So, if you are the type that loves talking about money, please be considerate and respect your partner's time. Never nag about money but talk about it in a very polite way. Although you may be the one taking charge or control of your family matters, you must find a way around it to avoid causing more harm than good to your relationship.

Never argue over money in your relationship rather, talk about it

Financial challenges or matters can be very disturbing to the point of creating serious argument or fight within a relationship. This has caused more debt, stress, and illnesses to some partners and the worst is death. If partners see each other as co-workers in the relationship, they should be able to avoid unnecessary arguments because of money matters.

Blaming and pointing fingers at each other about money can be devastating to family members. You should never allow blame-gaming ruin your relationship.

Partners should come to terms with accepting where and what the issues are and to resolve them without nagging and complaining over spilt milk. You either deal with it or allow it to cause more problems in your relationship.

Money matters are one of the main subjects most couples fight about_in their relationships. This can have serious and direct consequences on how couples live a happy life without being stressed out. Therefore, the attitude both partners have in regard to the spending and saving of money will determine how they enjoy their union together or separately. Couples who want to be happy in their relationships when it comes to financial matters must set some financial targets to the benefit of their relationship.

My wife and I sat down and agreed that until the bills are paid, we are not going to spend money on impulse buying no matter how desperate we think we need them. We both consult each other before spending money on things. Everything is budgeted and accounted for. We have a budget now on how we spend our money because some years back, we wasted money and now we have realised our mistakes. Therefore, as couples, you must both agree to save and spend money wisely. During the years that my wife and I made wrong financial decisions, we became broke.

Now, we have learned our lessons the hard way not to spend our money on the wrong things and on the wrong relationships.

Now that we handle our finances with care, I have been on mission trips to Ghana, South Africa and other places without stress of money and my wife has been to Ghana twice to visit her family. This is what happens when couples learn to spend and save money sensibly.

We all need encouragement to improve in life. So if your partner is the type of person who lacks financial management, then you must be ready to encourage or motivate him or her to improve and change their spending habits.

It takes a great team spirit to build a solid financial foundation in a relationship. Partners should see each other as a team player and develop means to empower them to get better. Good team players never let each other down but find ways to inspire each other toward a common goal. Relationship is team work. Therefore, couples should collaborate with each other and build a solid team.

Talk about your finances and never allow an argument to create negative and hostile conditions in your relationships. There is nothing worse than being in a relationship where you can't talk about everything.

Trust is built between partners when money issues are dealt with. Couples become more willing to understand each other and commit to things that will work in the relationship. They become fully aware about their financial situations and are honest about how they can both work together to resolve any longstanding problem caused by financial mismanagement. Nobody hides their payslip or financial statement but are honest and opened about their incomes including their personal investments. It is my wish that partners learn to work together and to avail themselves to talk about money matters as often as they can to prevent unforeseen debts.

It is time to talk about money matters before your relationship is destroyed.

Chapter Three

LET'S TALK ABOUT SEX BABE
(MARRIAGE COUPLES ONLY)

The husband should fulfil his wife's sexual needs, and the wife should fulfil her husband's needs. The wife gives authority over her body to her husband, and the husband gives authority over his body to his wife (1 Corinthians 7:3-5).

Sex is created by God to allow us to reproduce our kind. However, it also has a lot of health benefits to the body. Our body nerves have the ability to receive sexual pleasure or signal during sex.

Sex in marriage is a good thing ordained and blessed by God Himself for marriage couples. But the question is; how often do marriage couples set time aside to talk about sex in their relationship?

As much as sex is good, it needs to be discussed and talked about like anything else in the marriage. It is very important that couples feel free and confident to talk about sex. Failure to do this may result in infidelity and destroy the marriage. However, we must never forget to understand that every person is different and has different ideology about sex; let alone talk about it. This means that both partners should be ready and bold to talk about sex to get a better understanding of how each person feels about it. Sex is created to be enjoyed and therefore not talking about it with your spouse will leave you frustrated.

> 66
> **Wisdom is the principal thing; therefore get wisdom: and with all thy getting get understanding**
>
> **PROVERBS 4:7**

Talking about sex allows you to express how you feel about your partner's body. It gives you the power to share ideas together as to how to improve upon it next time.

Sex is a form of communication. Talking to your partner about sex should not be seen as a taboo. Nothing happens or improves by chance. Having a good or great sex life is not a miracle that will happen overnight. It must be talked about for it to get better.

If you want a great sex, then talk about it

My wife and I have been married for twelve years (coming September, 2016), and I can tell you that not all the sexual activities we have had over the years were great. With the pressure of working and further studies, sometimes, we hardly had sex less alone to find the time to talk about it.

We both understood the nature of our working time and other commitments during those periods and have learnt to adapt to it. It does not mean it is good; but we still create time to fulfil that aspect of our marriage. My wife is very good when it comes to talking about sex whiles I am good at performing the act. Hahaha! I am sure you are laughing right now.

This is what relationship is about. Complementing and sharing ideas as to what is best for you and working for both parties.

For you to have a level of great relationship with your partner, no stone should be left unturned. Whoever wants to talk about sex must be bold enough to inform the other partner about it so that time is made for that discussion. Never shy away from talking about sexual matters with your spouse. It helps to rebuild some cracks or broken bridges in the marriage. These days, people have become busy with life to the point that they hardly see each other for weeks or months. Whatever the case is for you, it is advisable to find time to talk about sex to avoid emotional damages or breakdown.

A sexless relationship is a vulnerable relationship

Talking about sex must not be done in a rush. Enough time must be allocated for it without any interruption from the children or phone calls. Deborah and I sometimes talk about sex on Fridays or when the children are in school. That time works best for both of us to discuss such delicate issues and other pressing matters that affect the marriage. We are able to resolve issues and regain energy to carry on in the marriage.

We have challenges within the marriage which every relationship is subject to go through but we learn to learn, unlearn and relearn how best we can make things work for us.

We used to be very angry and defensive at any little thing just because the underlying problem had not been dealt with, and that is sex. Talking about sex matters with your spouse allows you to exercise listening skills. You are more alert and eager to hear what is on the bed menu. Your mind and heart are opened to hear and learn from your partner as to what makes him or her happy about your sexual life.

Don't make excuses for not talking about sex. Be ready to talk, to listen and to learn

Sexual pleasures or fulfilments within the relationship require a lot of talking and listening. When you talk about sex, it drives away negative and suspicious thoughts against each other and prepares your mind for greater sexual activities. You are more able to turn your negative thoughts into a positive expectation of your partner.

A sexual activity within marriage is meant to be a passionate experience especially when a lot of talks go into it. However, it can be of a great deal for some spouses because none of them has the courage to break the ice and talk about sex.

Ignorance about sex can kill the passion you have for your partner

Sexual activities have the potential to bind couples even in difficult moments. Talking about it therefore brings you closer to your partner not only physically but emotionally. You become protective of your partner and his or her emotional wellbeing.

As we grow as humans, our body, desires and expectations change. These changes do have effect on our sexual relationships. Sometimes, illness or disease can limit the sexual drive we had for our partners and if it is not discussed thoroughly, it will break the marriage.

Talking to your partner about sex allows them to understand what those changes are and how to cope without feeling neglected or snubbed. As you are aware, this book is designed to encourage you about optimal sexuality within your relationship and to focus on how to improve your communication as couples in every area.

Talking to your partner about sex in the relationship helps them to understand your worries or concerns about your sexuality. This allows them to accept, appreciate and value you for whom you are and not what they have assumed over the years. You must be able to talk about the styles you want, how you want it in bed, how long you want it, and the places you want touched. For example, you must be able to talk about having sex in the bathroom or on the sofa. If this is what makes you happy and fulfilled, then why not? Talk about it!!

Some partners shy away from talking to their partners about how they feel health-wise. Hence, staying away from their partner. When this happens, the other partner may think they are being ignored or cheated on. This is why talking about the changes that occur to us as couples helps to prevent negative thoughts and promote healthy support for each other.

Our partners are not mind readers. Therefore, we must not expect them to read or know what is happening to us at a particular time. We owe it to them by explaining how we feel and the changes that are occurring about how we feel sexually. Some of these changes can be physical or emotional.

Whatever it is, we should be able to talk about it without fear to help settle our partners or remove doubt from their mind. Doing this ignites the passion we have always had for our partners and restores closeness and unity to build our self-esteem about sexual matters.

Bad sexual communication can affect the stability of a relationship. So, it will be wise to advice that whatever happens within the relationship must be talked about. Couples should never use silent treatment to score points. Each partner is entitled to feel great during sex. So if there is an issue that needs to be discussed, it must be discussed before sex time.

You should never feel bad telling your partner what you like. Be clear on what exactly you want in the act to determine your pleasure. Be honest and upfront about it. This is how you are taken seriously and heard. Talking about sex wouldn't harm your relationship but not talking about it may destroy it.

Most often, when a person hasn't had sex for some time, he or she may be embarrassed and think he or she has lost the power to function again. Talking about sex to your partner about your concerns may help to ignite your sexual drive. Be bold and confident about talking about sex; maybe that is what is on your partner's mind too.

Talk about sex to spice up your relationship.

WARNING: NO RING, NO SEX.

Chapter Four

WHAT IS THE PURPOSE
OF YOUR RELATIONSHIP?

"And the LORD God said, it is not good that the man should be alone; I will make him a help meet for him." Genesis 2:18

Have you thought about why you are in a relationship?

Many people have their own reasons for entering a relationship. Some reasons could be that; they want to be loved, cared for or get rich quick or on another hand, some may want to get into a relationship to express love, have more sex, share time together to avoid them being lonely, or to have someone with whom they can feel connected to.

Whatever reasons people may give as reasons to being in a relationship, it is very important that they both discover the main purpose for that relationship.

Just like anything created by God, every relationship is created to serve a purpose. That is why it will be detrimental to compare your relationship with other people's relationship. There is a reason and a purpose for your relationship and until you discover it, you will always hit your heads against the wall as couples.

When purpose is unknown, there will be abuse in the relationship. No relationship is programmed to fail but when the purpose for a relationship is not discovered, it makes it harder to maintain and live together.

Sadly, majority of people live together as couples without taking the pain to know or discover what actually makes relationships successful or fail. This chapter is to throw more light on the importance of knowing the purpose of your relationship.

Relationship has the power to make or break you

This is the more reason why people need to be very careful in choosing their life partners because whatever choices we make will determine the success or failure of the relationship. You are either being helped or hindered in your relationship because of the purpose you have discovered or failed to discover.

Are you being helped or hindered from discovering your full potential in your relationship?

God created everyone with a specific purpose. He expects us to live to fulfil that purpose in our lives, whether we are married or not. As couples, it is our respective duty to assist each other to discover and live that purpose. God knows that a man cannot or may not achieve that purpose alone so He made a helper for him to assist him to live that very purpose through companionship, knowledge, and faith.

You can never know about someone unless you develop companionship with them. This helps you to know how they behave and live their life. With this in mind, your faith in that person grows and develops as the relationship grows.

Having a good relationship with your partner can be very great but it requires commitment and dedication.

This however takes time but once each partner understands, it makes it easier to continue to chisel the best out of the relationship. When a purpose is discovered within a relationship, couples develop affection and love for each other knowing very well that they both need each other to achieve a common goal.

Couples develop patience, forbearance, compassion, love, joy, peace, kindness, goodness, faithfulness, gentleness and self-control for each other and help to develop one's ability to communicate and understand each other without fear of being seen as controlling or abusive when a purpose for the relationship is known.

Love is the foundation on which successful relationship is built.

A relationship that has discovered its purpose can help to make each partner a better person not only for relationship but also for the community they live in.

When both partners understand that they are not perfect but are ready to help each other's flaws and push each other to become a better person to achieve greater results, there is fulfilment.

It is never okay to be abusive in a relationship

"When purpose is unknown, abuse is inevitable." Myles Munroe

It is very shocking how some people think abusing their partners is okay. It is not. However, this kind of abuse happens in most relationships where a partner fails to discover the purpose for them living or coming together. A relationship where couples find it okay to abuse each other can be very detrimental to their own health and safety. This type of abuse can be in a form of silent treatment, passing negative remarks, withholding affection or sex, refusing to talk, threatening to leave, among others. These have the potential to destroy one's health in the long run. Couples who have discovered their purpose and want to continue in their long-term relationships should never entertain any form of abuse.

Nobody has the licence or certificate to be abusive to their partner

Relationship is not a prison and must not be treated as one. Everybody deserves to have a level of freedom in life and more so, in a relationship. Couples should learn to give their partners the freedom they deserve.

Sometimes, due to people's background and upbringing, they may want to have time for themselves without being interrupted by their partners.

It is very important that each couple understands that it is fine for them to have their space if needed. This is not a space to do anything silly or against their relationship but one to do the things that amuse them.

When this is understood and accepted, it helps to build a healthier and stronger union among partners.

Under no circumstances must a partner control his or her partner from having a space for themselves. Not allowing your partner to have a freedom of space to do what he or she loves can have a serious knock on the stability of your relationship. Couples should know that nobody likes others breathing down their neck. So they should learn to give them the space they crave for.

For every tree to grow and bear much fruits, that tree needs space to develop and flourish. This is not different from our relationships. For every relationship to flourish and fulfil destiny, couples need to give each other enough space to learn, grow, and explore as individuals. This is the reason why partners should never get in each other's way to the point of limiting their progress in life. Whatever you do as a couple, never deny each other the freedom to learn, relearn and unlearn (grow and develop).

Relationships are supposed to enhance and bring the best out of us. However, any relationship that leaves us feeling unworthy and unsure of ourselves is not good for us. A healthy and happy relationship should give each partner the chance to grow and develop in their area of passion and dreams.

It should provide a platform where each partner is able to exercise their freedom to achieve a dream without being restricted and controlled, undermined, belittled or demoralised. A relationship in which partners do not grow together will stagnate in life. Growing and achieving together as a couple help to promote sincerity and trust. Give room for your partner to develop the purpose why they are in your life.

When a couple has a purpose for their relationship, it goes a long way to empower, motivate and set them both on the journey of life. This keeps their relationship fresh and blossom. It is very important that that purpose propels you to achieve your family goals, dreams, and aspirations.

A couple with a good team spirit is able to achieve more and go beyond the walls (Egos, selfishness, jealousy, etc...) that have the potential to stop them from going forward in life.

The purpose of God for our relationships is to dwell in peace, patience and unconditional love for each other. This helps us to grow and discover the love of God for us and helping us to bring our relationships into the same level of understanding and respect for each other.

We all have emotions and, sometimes, they can have a toll on our relationship. Couples who have the purpose to support each other in all things must be ready to support each partner in their time of emotional breakdown; bearing in mind that there is no relationship without emotional challenges.

Our attitude towards each other is what gives us the platform to overcome doubt, hurt, jealousy, hatred or sadness as a result of emotional breakdown and free to talk about challenges openly with honesty and sincerity.

An untended garden develops weeds that destroy the plants

Our relationships are not different from a garden. When we fail to attend to the challenges that show up in our relationships, they create unwanted tension and destroy our beautiful relationships

(Garden). This is one of the reasons why it is important to talk about things (challenges) immediately. No good relationship just happens naturally just as not any beautiful garden springs forth without care. Couples who want to succeed together and grow well must learn to spend time to work on their relationship. Ignoring and not spend time talking about your relationship's purpose daily will only destroy your relationship.

Happiness in life comes as a result of moving forward in whatever you do as a couple. Couples who really want to experience unlimited happiness in their relationship must work together to move forward with their relationship. You cannot make any progressive move as couples when there is division of purpose. Your relationship's purpose must drive you both to the same direction or destination.

The question now is: how can couples motivate, encourage, inspire and provide unlimited support to each in order to achieve their respective purpose and relationship purpose?

Be in alignment with each other. Couples that agree together achieve much for their labour. To achieve your family dreams and purposes, you must both be in alignment or agreement.

A vehicle can't be on the road if the wheels are not in alignment

So are our relationships. We must learn to do things in agreement. We must not or should not do anything in disagreement; doing that will only destroy the joy and peace within the relationship. Security and confidence build up when we align or agree together and we achieve greater success within our relationships.

You can't achieve something that goes against your values and purposes as couples. Therefore as couples, you must work on your relationship's purpose and build yourself up together. Your relationship has a bright future.

Chapter Five

DON'T LET WORRY, ANXIETY AND INSECURITY RUIN YOUR RELATIONSHIP

Are you allowing worry, anxiety and insecurity to destroy your relationship? Perhaps, some of us are possibly ruining our relationship without knowing. When we allow these elements into our relationships, they eat the fabric of the relationship and destroy it.

Having a good relationship with our partners is about sharing everything we have to bring happiness in the relationship. This helps us to grow and bond in love and unity.

As much as we love our partners, allowing anxiety, worries and insecurity can have a serious damage on our relationships. We must never forget that none of us is perfect and we mustn't expect perfection from our partners.

One of the most pleasurable things in the world is relationships. We all need it to survive. However, getting into the wrong type of relationship can destroy one's destiny forever. A wrong relationship can be likened to a prison where partners are stacked or locked up in their emotions and worries. This can easily be a breeding ground for stagnation, failure, health challenges, depression and possible death.

Any relationship that has allowed jealousy and insecurity to control its direction may not survive for long. Worry, anxiety and insecurity are like acid that have the potential to destroy any good and happy relationship no matter those involved.

When these three demons are allowed to enter our relationships, they create vacuum of loneliness, isolation and distance between us as couples; thus generating negative thoughts about each other and forcing happy relationships to crumble and die.

Anxiety, worry and insecurity in relationships come in various ways and it is very important that couples learn to identify and deal with the root cause of these demons in their relationships.

These relationship demons can make couples turn against each other for no apparent reasons; creating negative feelings and hostile behaviours toward each other. When this happens, couples begin to lose hope, faith, trust, love and support for each other. This can also lead to low self-esteem and respect within the relationship. In fact, it generates negative and evil thoughts that undermine the success and support of the relationship which then leads to other health challenges like depression, stress, hypertension and paranoia.

These demons can make you plan evil against your partner and unnecessarily making you act like a mad horse trying to pull down a house. One becomes overly angry and frustrated when insecurity sets into their mind and become furious or upset with their partner for even coming home late for dinner. Instead of couples enjoying their good and precious moments together, they waste their whole day or night arguing and tearing each other apart like a lion devouring its prey.

Worry, anxiety and insecurity pose as demons to most relationship success. They act like poison, slowing down couples from pursuing the plans and ambitions they have. Worry and anxiety have the potential to destabilise your ability to focus in life and to have a clear emotional, mental, spiritual and a physical desire to remain resolute in the pursuit of success; affecting your thinking power to see positivity in life

These relationship demons create negative pictures in couples' mind which then go a long way to limit and prevent them from seeing positivity in every positive step into achieving greatness in life by diverting, distracting, and preoccupying them with pressure.

Worry becomes inevitable when one shifts their focus from positive steps to the negative; making them feel let down and stressed. These demons do not only affect our thoughts but attack our emotions; they destroy us from within if it is not dealt with from the onset.

They have no respect for anybody, status, race, gender, or height. These demons affect even the poor and have the potential to break barriers just to affect their ability to change their situations. I have noticed that these relationship demons have a pragmatic effect on their victims and limit them from achieving their goals and purpose in life by sucking their joy and happiness in achieving something great and significant.

The effects of these relationship demons can be very devastating to one's destiny. They pose a threat to our self-esteem, confidence and courage in the pursuit of success. They can be equated to airborne diseases which have no boundaries. Therefore, we need to be aware of these bugs as we pursue success in life.

Most often it is impossible to think clearly when our life is flooded and choked with anxiety. One of the best things couples can do to overcome worry, anxiety and insecurity is to try and take their time out to relax their mind so as to regain energy to chase their dreams. When they are able to do this, they feel better once again and make positive decisions in life.

I have observed that when people are depressed or anxious about something, their whole life gets affected, limiting their ability to think or make rational decisions regarding their life. Anxiety affects the family, social, emotional, biological and spiritual wellbeing of the individual. It changes and creates negative moods which affect our relationships, personal appearance, and daily interests. It sometimes goes a long way to breakdown the loving family union one might have had.

These demons have the capacity or ability to affect one's desire to motivate him or her to pursue success in life because of the toxics bugs they leave behind such as fatigue, poor sleep, aches and pains, leading to lack of energy for everyday duties or excessive exhaustion after small amounts of activity. Most often, individuals who get affected by these demons express low self-confidence, lose interest in hobbies making them to isolate themselves from others or social activities

Being a public health professional and a lifestyle coach, I have discovered that when a person suffers from depression or severe anxiety, it can lead to suicidal thoughts. This can affect anyone; from a child to an adult. Suicidal thoughts and death can be a major symptom of anxiety and must be taken very seriously. Anyone affected by anxiety is likely to feel worthless and the only option they think they have is to take their life.

Anxiety is caused by the people we surround ourselves with as couples. Sometimes, people over-expect from us and if we are unable to meet their expectations, we get upset and allow fear to set in to choke our spirit of greatness.

You have the power to detach from these individuals as couples because our success demands that we acknowledge our strength and avoid being stressed out by the options presented us, and the expectations of people and never accepting the opinion of others to be our perfection in our relationship.

In order to challenge and deal with these relationship demons (anxiety, worry and insecurity), couples must learn to discover themselves and their strengths as individuals. This enables them to believe in themselves and do not rely on their partners for self-approval. Ignorance about oneself is what creates worry, anxiety and insecurity within the relationship. Once couples discover who they are in their relationship, they are able to find their respective purpose and take steps to make things work in their relationships regardless of the challenges that may oppose them.

Fear, worry and insecurity will never find their way into our relationship when we discover ourselves. We cannot help our partners when we have not discovered our personal strengths and weaknesses.

Every relationship has their own demons that show up sometimes to cause division or separation but when each couple becomes aware of these demons, they can overcome them easily.

Many things in life are subject to change because life itself changes. But if couples make up their mind to remain steadfast in the face of all these changes, regardless of the stage of their relationships, they can surely overcome, rebuild and keep moving their relationship forward to the next level by the choices and decisions they make.

These demons destroy any solid and happy relationship. Don't let them ruin your relationship. Couples should not forget that each of them has something they are or can be afraid of in life or in the relationship.

Therefore, couples should create the room to talk about anxiety, worry and insecurity without intimidation. Once this is done, they will begin to feel accepted, understood, and most importantly, help each other to deal with all these little foxes that might destroy the relationship. Talk about them as soon as they show their ugly faces. Your relationship is bound to succeed.

TALK ABOUT IT, WORK AT IT AND SUCCEED IN IT. KEEP TALKING

Chapter Six

ARE YOUR FRIENDS RUINING YOUR RELATIONSHIP?

Talk About It

Having other people in your relationship can be very beneficial to its growth, development, and acceleration. Some friends come in to provide support, advice, etc. However, some of these friends come in to limit, kill, steal and destroy your relationship.

Some of these friends could be your church members, work colleagues, social club or media friends who out of jealousy and envy will do everything possible to destroy the relationship you have with your partner.

Most often, they are friends who know you very well and can tell the world about your childhood. Allowing such individuals into your life can damage every fabric of your marriage or relationship.

Please, I am not undermining the value of friendship in our relationships, but the issue is that getting it wrong can have a devastating blow to your relationship. No matter how sweet and happy our relationships are with our partners, we should never neglect the value and importance of friends to us.

Friends will always remain part of us as couples but we need to be very careful of those we allow into our relationships. Under no circumstance should we place our friends above our partners regardless of their connection or association to us. We should be very watchful of our behaviours and not allow them to dominate and control us.

As couples, it is vital that we never allow too much freedom and easy access to friends especially when it comes to our personal relationship with our spouse. This is because, out of envy, some of these friends can sow seeds of argument, fight, and betrayal into our relationship causing it to breakdown.

Allowing closeness and freedom to some friends can prevent our relationship from growing and bearing much fruits. This alone can cause a whole lot of family challenges, rifts and interferences within our marriages. This means that, couples need to talk about their friends and avoid or get rid of those who have the potential to destroy their marriage or relationship out of jealousy and envy.

It takes a lot to build a solid and great relationship with our spouses. As such, every second must be used to flush out negative friends that may pose as a threat to the success of our marriages.

Some friends can be very funny, dangerous, and creepy. They can leech into your relationship and cause havoc to it beyond remedy. As couples, we need to identify which of our friends have the tendency to manipulate or create unbearable situations for us and avoid them. Friends must be kept as friends, not advisers or directors of your relationship. They do not have the licence to dictate or control your affairs as couples. So, if you both identify that a friend is posing challenges to your relationship, you must put a stop to it immediately before your marriage or relationship is destroyed.

Some of these friends can make you feel belittled about yourself or unhappy about your partner. You have to mark them and avoid them. *Now I beseech you, brethren, mark them which cause divisions and offences contrary to the doctrine which ye have learned; and avoid them* (**Romans 16:17**).

Out of jealousy and envy, some friends can create negativity between couples by gossiping or lying about things they are not sure about. This can easily create division among couples. Couples must be very careful and watchful of these characters or behaviours of their friends and never jump into conclusion or assumptions about their partner.

I would rather encourage couples to stick together to address any misbehaviour from any of their friends and ensure that that individual is warned or removed from the relationship.

A good, healthy friendship should be one that promotes positivity among partners, and supporting them to stand together in love and harmony in order to have a happy home. Good friends will do everything possible to ensure that everything about the couple is going on well without feeling or desiring to be the one in the relationship. On the other hand, some of these friends can sabotage your relationship out of envy by undermining your partner's way of living, dressing, cooking or reasoning. This causes friction among partners and sends the relationship packing. This type of friends must never be entertained within the family home. They are very dangerous to the cell of the relationship. Avoid these types of friends at all cost before your relationship is destroyed.

When we allow a jealous person or friend around us, they create all sorts of resentment against ourselves or our partners. When this happens, couples start to behave hostilely against each other because someone has a problem seeing them live happily. Some friends may have issues with your partner but will not say in the open but will do things to disrespect him or her. As couples, identify and deal with such behaviour. Never create room to accommodate such behaviours.

In fact, dealing with jealous friends can be difficult, especially if these friends have been very supportive or played a big role in your relationship, but no matter how hard it seems, both partners should stand together to address these friends before their relationship is destroyed.

Never try to deal with friends who seem to be creating issues for your relationship alone. It is very important that whichever friend is causing the issues is called by both partners to address issues amicably.

I have no doubt in my mind that friends play very important roles in building our relationships but there are few of them out there who do not care about the happiness of our relationship and we must do everything possible to send them packing.

Personally, I have had some old friends who stood with me during my marriage to my wife and they are still around till date. We are like family with them. However, it does not mean that we go to their homes to wreck or destroy the harmonious relationship they have with their partners just because of being friends.

As friends, we have contributed to enrich each family both spiritually, financially, materially and socially. This is what friendship is about. We have been there for them, providing, promoting and maintaining healthy friendship.

Over the years, we have celebrated good times together as couples, and providing support during bad times especially when Deborah's mum passed on. These friends stood with us and ensured that we were fine and well. They even offered some financial help. What a friendship!

Not everyone can provide us with the needed support we need as couples when we need it. So every partner should turn to their partner for support rather than turning to friends who may not be happy with their partners. Confiding in these friends about your marriage or relationship will only create trouble for the relationship instead of providing solution to it.

> **He who walks with wise men will be wise, but the companion of fools will suffer harm.**
>
> **PROVERBS 13:20**

Let us face it: sometimes the people we call friends can be difficult to deal with. Some of these friends do not care about how we feel about our relationship with our partners but have the audacity to speak evil about our partners or stab us in the back just to win the attention of our partners. Their purpose is to cause trouble for our relationship in order for them to snatch it.

Some of the people we call friends get very threatened that we are enjoying happy and peaceful relationship with our partners so they intentionally create negative thoughts in our minds about our partners just to see the relationship crumble.

They suddenly spread negative rumours about you or your partners just for you to start a fight and break away. Such friends should be given the red card and not given a chance around your marriage or relationship.

One thing we must never forget is that relationship with those outside our marriages have the potential to make or break our marriages. Therefore, couples must create time to talk about their friends or associations who they allow into their marriages. This can help to build trust between a couple and bring unity in the family. Not everyone wants to see your relationship work or last so, as couples, it is your collective duty to ensure that no friend is allowed to sow seeds of division and separation within your relationship. Nothing is more dangerous than allowing a toxic friend to leech his or her teeth onto your relationship.

It is never too late to build new friends around your relationship as couples. But, it will be very beneficial if you can avoid every Tom, Dick, and Harry to come into your relationship to destroy it.

Chapter Seven

IS SOCIAL MEDIA RUINING YOUR RELATIONSHIP?

Talk About It

It is shocking to discover how flirting seems to be easy these days. The reason for this is because of the rate at which technology and the Internet have increased in our society. Many people are now using mobile phones, laptops or other smart devices. These gadgets have contributed to the breakdown of effective communication between couples. They however promoting flirtatious habits with other opposite sex over the Internet especially on social media.

In this chapter, we will look at how social media and the Internet have contributed to the breakdown of effective communication within relationships.

There is no doubt that social media has contributed a lot in the development of social structures, helping in education and increasing of knowledge. However, it has also played a massive role in family breakdown.

Although some may argue that social media can be a substitute to real life relationships, it can also be argued that valuable time could be used to develop or form real relationships and build effective communication among couples instead of allowing social media to occupy those valuable times.

Over the years, we have all communicated verbally and nonverbally thus allowing face to face interaction and conversation. Nowadays, recent improvements in technology and Internet have shifted the mode of communication among couples and contributed to isolation.

Prior to the writing of this chapter, I spoke to some ten couples regarding this subject and eight out of the ten agreed that social media has affected the way they communicate within their relationship but two out of the ten said they never use social media and therefore, they have managed their marital relationship perfectly.

From personal observation, social media affect the way couples interact or behave towards each other in a relationship especially where it has taken the centre of the relationship.

It is very necessary that couples talk about this aspect of their relationship and never overlook it when it is causing breakdown within the family home.

Although the usage of social media can be seen as a tool for reducing and eliminating loneliness, it can also be a tool for destroying relationships.

These, on other hand, create unnecessary arguments between a couple. A partner can easily get jealous of their partner for using social media too much and he or she may feel intimidated, isolated and ignored in the relationship which may lead to the breakdown of communication, and hinder the growth of the relationship.

Too much of everything can be very destructive to us as human beings and social media is not exempted. It is advised that couples learn to discuss any challenges arising because of social media that may hamper the stability of the relationship.

Couples should be able to spend valuable time together and must be free to express the disapproval of time a partner spends on social media.

It is important that couples value and respect the time they spend together especially when they are home. They must never allow the distraction of social media take their focus and attention off each other.

People are different and interact differently to things. Therefore, if a partner does not like to use any social media, he or she must not control or prevent their partner from using it.

A partner may get so worried or disturbed about the sort of information the other partner shares on social media and that could be a starting point for trouble and argument.

When this happens, it will be inappropriate to get confrontational with your partner. Rather, find time to talk about your feelings amicably or both partners can devise other means of how the issue can be resolved.

Relationship is meant to be enjoyed between husband and wife sharing good time without a third party. Allowing social media in your relationship can easily contribute to breakdown or divorce especially when one is found to be cheating on their partner.

It will be better and wise to be self-aware or alert of the potential damages social media could have on the relationship and avoid it. Never allow social media to control your relationship. Take control of it before your relationship is destroyed. Business couples must endeavour to explain to each other the importance of their using social media for business purposes but should not allow it to drag the relationship into dispute.

As a lifestyle coach and writer, I use social media a lot to reach out to clients or mentees who need to speak with me but cannot come to my house. I use Facebook a lot to promote my books and other events that I deem necessary to invite others to attend. However, I do not overdo it. I limit the time I spend on Facebook, Twitter and WhatsApp.

This is because I try to spend quality time with my family especially the children to do their home work, reading and other family outing such as going to the cinema or visiting friends.

This has made my life very easy and smooth without any argument or creating an idea in my wife's head. Although sometimes I struggle to maintain this technique, I try not to allow it to control my relationship with my family.

There is always time for everything. Therefore, couples should never use their family times to be on social media. Family time is family time. You cannot save the whole world and leave or break your family union. So, it is dangerous to spend more time on social media and neglect your partner or family.

A relationship without trust can never stand

It is crucial that couples learn to trust each other when it comes to social media. We should never forget that we are individuals. Some people are very introvert whiles others are extrovert.

This means that a partner could be very opened about how he or she deals with his or her social media status. The other partner should be able to understand and do not control the partner from using social media when there is trust.

This goes a long way to prevent jealousy, insecurity, and doubt against each other. This can't be possible without partners finding time to talk about it.

Social media has a way of ruining relationships regardless of how long partners have known each other. Couples should be very informed about the dangers of this killer bug and take the necessary steps to stamp it out from ruining their relationship.

Sometimes, a partner may compare his or her partner to someone they have seen on social media. This can be very devastating to the relationship especially when that person is known to the couple.

People look and show their love in different ways. So seeing them on social media does not mean they are better than you or your partner. Couples must learn to appreciate each other regardless of look or appearance. Nobody can ever be like your partner neither will there be anyone like you. Love and appreciate your partner for whom they are.

Friends on social media could be showing interest in you or your partner but may never tell you. So comparing your relationship or partner with them only gives them the winning power to want to create competition for your partner. Remember that no relationship is perfect but it can be worked at. No matter how difficult or tempting it is to you as couples, never compare your relationship with anyone else's.

Social media and technology can be very addictive and if a partner lacks self-discipline or self-control, he or she will be opening the back door for problems and challenges to break and destroy the relationship.

When couples discover and know their purposes for their relationship, they are able to encourage and remind each other that their happiness does not depend on other people's happiness.

Never allow social media relationships with others destroy your relationship. Instead of allowing unnecessary envy, hatred, and jealousy, prevent your relationship from making progress, begin to empower, encourage, motivate and inspire each other to achieve the best relationship you can both have as a couple.

Couples should find time to communicate more than ever to allow for stronger and healthier relationships. When this happens, it empowers, encourages, and motivates partners to stay together without fear of losing each other.

Let jealousy and undermining of each other because of social media get out of the window and build love and respect. Whatever it is, learn to put your smart gadgets off and don't let social media ruin your relationship. Social media has destroyed some lovely relationships because some couples have been found cheating in bed with other friends of the opposite sex who they met on social media. When these couples got married, they were best friends without technology and social media.

However, since the inception of social media and smart gadgets, couples are no more talking to see how best they can improve their relationship. Some couples are just too busy looking at the images of other people over the Internet, enjoying online dating but avoiding real relationship with their partners.

High Internet use may lead to conflict, breakdown, and misunderstanding between couples. Some partners may be addicted to chatting and flirting on the Internet with some strange individuals hence jeopardising their relationships with their partners.

Cheating or infidelity is not anything new to mankind but amazingly, social media has contributed to make it more rampant among couples. It is therefore necessary that couples learn and find the right time to speak about how social media have or is affecting their relationship without fear. Talk about it in order to sustain and keep your relationship.

Chapter Eight

IS SNORING AFFECTING YOUR RELATIONSHIP?

Talk About It

Just like any health challenge that affects us human beings and has impact on our relationships, snoring is not an isolated case. Snoring can have great impact on your relationship with your spouse. It can affect the way couples share happy and great night sleep together in bed or cause sleep deprivation.

Everybody needs a good sleep after a busy day at work. As such, they don't want to be deprived from a sound sleep by anyone including their partner. When this happens, it can lead to tiredness and fatigue due to less sleep, irritability, and increased health challenges for some partners because a partner keeps his or her significant other awake throughout the night leading to them experiencing less effectiveness at work or during the day.

Give each other space to breath in the relationship

Therefore, if this has become an issue within the relationship, then, couples should talk about it and see how best they can address this challenge. Couples should not throw in the towel or break their relationship just because snoring has become the elephant in the relationship.

Talking about it and seeking medical solution to it is the best way forward in dealing with this challenge that could potentially deprive your partner from having sound sleep at night.

Snoring is a medical condition that can be addressed. Therefore, do not allow that to ruin your relationship. According to some medical experts, "Snoring is caused by the vibration of soft tissue in your head and neck as you breathe in and out during sleep" (NHS Choices).

It is suggested that people who snore have their airways relax and narrow while sleeping which affects air pressure within their airways and causes the tissue to vibrate. This leads to their airways being blocked partially.

What is snoring and how does it affect our relationships?

"Snoring happens when you can't move air freely through your nose and throat during sleep. This makes the surrounding tissues vibrate which produce the familiar snoring sound. People who snore often have too much throat and nasal tissue or "floppy" tissue that is more prone to vibrate. The position of your tongue can also get in the way of smooth breathing (NHS Choices).

The wife of a friend of mine snores a lot and previously, it disturbed and deprived him of having sound sleep at night, but he spoke with me about the issue and as a public health advisor, I encouraged him to find the right time and moment to discuss it with her and also to find ways of dealing with it. He has become more accommodative and tolerant of his wife's snoring. He has no doubt that he may snore but his wife's is just too much to the point that they sought medical intervention for her condition.

In my work as a public health professional, I have discovered that snoring can be a sign of breathing problems which may be affecting the airways thus causing sleeplessness or sleep apnoea which medical attention must be sought to diagnose the underlying factors contributing to the snoring.

Just like any medical condition, snoring can easily contribute to some relationship break down if it is not addressed and dealt with properly.

Four years into their marriage, he noticed that his wife's snoring was just becoming too much for him to bear and because he didn't want to create unnecessary tension that may affect the relationship, he opted to sleep in the children's room. What even made it easier for him was that he requested night duties at work most of the time just to avoid being disturbed by her snoring.

As couples, sharing the same bed plays a vital role in bonding but having one person snoring during that intimate moment can limit the bonding aspect of the relationship. This has the potential to put undue pressure on the relationship and create isolation.

Therefore, it is wise to talk about how your partner's snoring affects your relationship and come to terms with how both of you can resolve it and still have peace at home especially in bed without having to fight for sound sleep after sex.

At first, it was difficult for him to address the issue of snoring with his wife but as it was getting too much for him to take, he asked to speak to her about it and pointed out how that has contributed to his tiredness and fatigue at home. Initially, he thought she would have been embarrassed to hear him talk about it but she was very receptive about it and they both came up with a solution best for them in order to enjoy a good night's sleep.

There are challenges in every relationship. These can be trivial or major matters. Regardless how these challenges are seen, they should be discussed and talked about only if couples value their relationship and want to move forward to make things work within the relationship.

Therefore in a relationship where a couple snores too much to the point of causing sleep deprivation to the other partner, both partners should rest assured that the issues can be solved so that both can have a peaceful and sound sleep.

Understanding your partner is the way forward into a happy relationship

I will suggest that if you are being disturbed or deprived from sleep due to the noise should learn to be more understanding of the uncontrollable challenges of your partner and never allow resentment or hurt fill him or her up to take unnecessary steps to destroy the relationship.

During those moments where my friend lacked an understanding of his wife's snoring condition, he had always slept in the children's room for many years which also resulted or developed other relationship issues and challenges for them. To him, it was the best solution to the snoring challenges at the time but as time and years went by, they were drifting apart to the point where the children now wanted to sleep in his bed rather than their own beds. This created separation, loneliness, and isolation within the relationship which was not healthy for them.

If snoring has found its way into your relationship and causing trouble for you as a couple, find the right and appropriate measures to talk about it before your relationship is destroyed.

Set a time as a priority to discuss the issues and see how best to find solutions to the snoring problem. This could be done by seeking medical intervention for a therapy to help resolve your partner's snoring issue. When this is done in a happy and understanding way, it will rather create oneness than breaking you apart. "Let's Talk About It Baby" should be your first approach in dealing with any relationship hurdle. It can be done. Just talk about it.

Chapter Ten

DON'T LET CONFLICT DESTROY YOUR RELATIONSHIP

Talk And Deal With It

Every relationship has its own storm to face. This storm is the conflict that challenges the relationship we have with our partners. No marriage is the same and must never be seen as such.

> 66
> "You can't stop the storm, but you can learn to soar above it."

Being ignorant about the fact that every relationship goes through a level of conflict is just denying that you exist in a real world. No matter how loving and caring couples become or look, there has been a conflict that has challenged them and made them stronger in their relationship.

Conflict in relationship comes as a result of couples having different levels of expectations, interests, personalities, backgrounds and habits which sometimes clash to create misunderstanding. However, these misunderstanding or conflict can be manageable and resolved if couples begin to identify or accept the reason and the causes of it.

Unresolved conflicts can easily lead to loneliness, stress, isolation, resentment, hurts and neglect within the relationship. As couples, we need to understand that conflicts are part of life and not there to damage or destroy our relationships.

Conflict is just like the storm. No one has the power to stop the storm from coming but can learn to soar above it. One of the ways to soar above the storm in a relationship is to develop the right attitude as couples to deal with it. Disagreements and misunderstanding will surely come into every relationship no matter how much couples claim to love each other but they are not to lead to divorce or painful separation.

When couples fail to resolve any form of conflict or challenges within their relationship, it can easily create hurdles against effective communication and limit the progress of the relationship because none of the couples wants to speak just in case it escalates into more serious issue. In fact, not being open about things will rather create an acidic and volatile environment for both couples. This is the main reason why couples must learn to talk about anything that is bothering them without fear.

When couples allow fear to prevent them from speaking openly about issues affecting them in the relationship, the issue turns into cancerous cells that eat the entire relationship to death.

Regardless of whom is wrong or right in the relationship, couples must learn to humble themselves and avoid pride to rule their heart to destroy the relationship.

> 66
> **"Let all bitterness, wrath, anger, clamour, and evil speaking be put away from you, with all malice"**
>
> **EPHESIANS 4:31**

Most often, we over expect from each other and that puts pressure on our partners. This creates conflict in the relationship. When we expect too much from our partners, we have the tendency to lose our tolerance for each other. Some couples get very upset and angry unnecessarily just because their partner may be reacting or behaving differently from what they want.

Couples must learn to be tolerant of each other bearing in mind that each and every one of them is different and may respond to things from a different level or perspective. Couples who talk about issues amicably have respect and value for each other. They value the input of each other in the relationship and encourage each other to contribute whatever that bothers them openly.

Couples who respect and talk about their conflict openly stand together. They enjoy the fruits of their labour as a family. The wife becomes very humble to the husband and the husband loves the wife without any reservations. Nobody sees him or herself as superior over the other. Mutual love and forgiveness are demonstrated easily.

If you realise that you are not able to forgive your partner easily, then you must check your relationship and see what actually is hurting you and talk about it. You must never allow arrogance and pride to stop you from forgiving your partner and speak about issues to find solution in order to move the relationship forward.

It is perfectly alright to discuss how you feel about your partner. This prevents resentment against your partner. When couples fail to talk about the little foxes that spoil the vine, it creates negative feelings toward each other because things are not spoken about truthfully and openly.

Couples must remember that conflicts are like foxes that will try to spoil their happiness, enjoyment and togetherness. Therefore, partners should discuss everything in love and respect. This goes a long way to enhance the purpose and project the good image of the relationship.

> **"Take us the foxes, the little foxes that spoil the vines: for our vines have tender grapes"**
>
> **SONG OF SOLOMON 2:15**

In order to achieve the purpose of coming together as a couple, each partner must learn to ask forgiveness whenever they go wrong. This will help partners to forgive easily without any form of unnecessary bitterness and anger. Partners should always think about each other and try to understand how the other partner feels about the conflict.

Humility is the bridge that puts couples together. A humble couple will put away pride and ask forgiveness for the things that he or she has done against his or her partner. Under no circumstances should a partner feel too proud to ask for forgiveness when they have gone wrong.

Each couple should learn to take control of their thoughts

Couples who want to continue to enjoy their relationships must learn never to live in past hurts. Hurts and disappointments will always come; but as couples, we should learn to let go.

Holding on to past hurts or regrets will only lead us to more regrets unless we are ready and prepared to let go and press on in resolving the conflict. It is totally pointless to hold grudges against your partner because it will not give you the free mind to move forward into fruitfulness.

> ❝
> **"And be ye kind one to another, tender-hearted, forgiving one another, even as God for Christ's sake hath forgiven you"**
>
> **EPHESIANS 4:32**

If we are willing to enjoy our relationships then we need to change our attitude and behaviour towards each other. As couples, you have to develop harmony among you regardless of the conflict that comes into the relationship. Couples should avoid blame game in the relationship. Blaming each other in the face of conflict will never help to resolve it; rather, it makes things worse.

Past conflicts can make it difficult for couples to live in the present of the relationship. Allowing hurt memories to control the relationship will make it difficult for couples to plan and prepare for the future of the relationship. Therefore, couples should let go of past hurts that prevent them from sharing loving moments together and make them unfulfilled.

No one can ever control the past but they can take full control of what they do and expect in the future. However, focusing on your partner's behaviour towards you will stop you from taking full control of your destiny as an individual and never allow the past hurt, anger or sorrow hold you captive.

Couples should not allow conflict to create isolation within the relationship but allow it to bind them in love, unity, and respect. They should be ready and prepared to speak about anything that troubles them.

Never allow guilt to control your relationship. Talk about it

I will suggest that couples do not waste their entire time and relationship dealing with conflict and challenges; rather, focus on ways you can help each other become the best partner. This can only be possible if both couples develop the habit of talking about any conflict that arises within the relationship. Nothing should hold you back from talking about it.

Chapter Eleven

HAVE YOU LOST YOUR AFFECTION?
(TALK ABOUT IT)

Lack of attraction leads to frustration

We all need affection in our lives and most importantly in our relationships and marriages. Just as water is good for plants' growth, affection is vital in the growth of every relationship.

No plant can survive without water. Water is an essential part for every living organism. Therefore, for a farmer who wants his or her plants to grow and bear much fruits, he or she must learn to water it.

Water plays four major roles in the development and growth of every plant. It helps to germinate seeds, helps in the process of photosynthesis by which plants prepare their food, transports nutrients and minerals from the soil to the plants, helps in the maintenance of plant and providing strength to the plant tissues.

Just as plants need water and our body needs regular balanced diet or nutritious meals to grow and survive, our relationships or marriages need affection to develop, grow and last longer.

Our relationships starve and die (fall apart) when we fail to give enough affection to our partners.

The grass will not get green until you water it. When we show affection to our partners, it helps to cement or glue the relationship together in love and harmony. Just as fuel is needed to carry a vehicle from point A to B, affection can be regarded as the fuel that pushes the relationship forward. Without affection in a relationship, couples stagnate and the relationship fails.

Affection promotes and provides security for the relationship. It is like a foundation of a building. Without a solid foundation, a building has no future. The building collapses when the foundation is not strong and solid enough to hold it when storm comes against it. This is what happens to our relationships when we lack affection for each other.

Lack of affection has the potential to hurt our relationships. It limits the level of intimacy couples have for each other and creates unnecessary stress, pressure and pain. It makes couples feel lonely, unloved, and undeserved

If your husband or wife is not showing much affection to you in the relationship, please find time to talk about it amicably. We shouldn't forget that we are all built differently and have different ways of expressing our love. However, if you are not sure about the love your partner is showing you, please, talk about it. Couples who learn to discuss or talk about things in their relationships live in intimacy and eliminate assumptions and doubts from their relationship.

It is also very important that when a husband or wife expresses how he or she feels, it is taken seriously and dealt with before it destroys the marriage. If a couple opens up regarding the causes of their mood or emotion about the way things are going in the relationship, the other partner should be helpful and caring enough to have time to listen. This could be something that may be destroying him or her. An atmosphere should be created for that partner to express him or herself freely without being seen as a nagger or complainer.

Affection promotes respect and appreciation in a relationship

Couples who express affection to each other enjoy respect and appreciation from each other. This is one of the ways couples enjoy long-lasting union.

Respecting and appreciation each other as couples prevent intimidation and undermining of each other especially in public places. They don't yell, raise or shout at each other, or become rude to each other. They understand the need or the place of respect in building a healthy and lovely relationship.

Respect is not commanded but given in order to attract it back. Therefore, when couples have affection for each other, they are able to respect each other for whom they are. Couples who respect each other are able to show support and value each other's independence or contribution in the relationship.

As we all know and understand, affection is something we all need especially from our partners. Therefore, if you are losing that affection for your husband or wife, please, talk about it and come to terms with reviving that affection for your partner.

Perhaps in the upbringing of your spouse, he or she was not taught how to show affection. Talking about this will help you to understand your partner and help them to develop or show you that affection you are looking for in your relationship.

If you are the one from whom your partner wants to regain affection, it is very important that you humble yourself to speak about it to your partner and let them help you to embark on the journey.

It does not take much to please our partners. It only takes simple things to rekindle the fire in the relationship.

I remember many years back I struggled to show affection to my wife in some areas and that was hurting her without my knowledge. My wife always says to me that she loves me and for many years, I have always answered her that, I know. Now, this was the way I grew up as a child who never heard my parents telling me how they loved me and cared about what I did. So I never knew how to respond to my wife. In the long run, it was a particular relationship conference we attended together in church. During the questions and answers session, my wife asked the question about how to handle a husband who never says he loves you but, says "I KNOW"

In fact, I felt very bad and learned my lesson from that day and began responding appropriately to her. We are not the perfect couple, but we have been enjoying our relationship since then.

Are you losing your affection for your partner? This is the time to talk about it. There could be simple things you can both do to revive affection for each other.

My wife now calls me "HONOURABLE" because I have learnt to show affection to her by responding affectionately to her when she tells me she loves me. Talking about things concerning how one feels about their partner helps to deal with blind spots preventing them from enjoying their union.

If you are looking for ways to regain affection from your partner, you could also begin to communicate your need specifically.

Maybe you are the one who loves hugging, kissing, cuddling, and holding of hands. You must be able to communicate that to your partner and never expect that change will occur overnight.

If you think or assume that you are losing affection for your partner, I would encourage you to talk about the issue with your partner. Let him or her understand how that affects you and solve it amicably so that others will not be affected.

Couples should learn to be frank with each other and express their feelings regardless of how difficult it may seem. It is better to talk about things in your relationship in private before they explode in public. Learn to communicate and revive your relationship by building the broken bridges of affection. It is possible things can work again in your relationship. Never give up on each other but talk about things. You can and must talk about it!

Chapter Twelve

ARE FAMILY MEMBERS DESTROYING YOUR RELATIONSHIP?

In life not everyone will be happy with you. People are not equal and that is the same in some family relationships. Sometimes we get into marriage or relationships expecting to be

> **"What therefore God has put together, let no man put asunder."**
>
> **MARK 10:9**

loved by our in-laws. Unfortunately, every member of the family may not be in good terms with you. It takes great effort to stay away from such family members who are constantly causing issues for your relationship.

No matter how challenging you try to make things work between you and some family members, they may still find fault with you or your partner. This can be very disturbing and frustrating if you don't know how to deal with such people in the family.

Nothing is frustrating in a relationship like having difficult and uncompromising in-laws

These individuals can be thorns in the flesh. Whatever you do to please them, they see it as not good enough. The danger is that not all partners are really in the place to deal with such controversial in-laws.

Instead of walking away peacefully, your partner may choose to face or address them squarely and if wisdom is not applied, it can lead to the breakdown of the relationship you have with your partner. So the question is: what do you do when family members seem to be ruining your relationship?

Do you allow them to continue or walk away from your relationship or talk about it with your partner?

My wife and I have been married for twelve years now and I must say that it hasn't been easy for us. We had to argue over a particular family member, threatening to leave the marriage, and even see each other as the problem instead of the family member as the root cause. This was not very healthy for us.

We were very bitter and angry at each other because of this family member we looked up to and thought we were obligated to allow into our marriage. We both suffered pain and hurt as a result. We saw that person as the one to lean on, call on, or have their counsel when we both needed it. We forgot that not all family members are genuine and honest with their approaches.

Not all family members are there to build your relationship. Some feel they own the success of the relationship because of the sacrifices they have made in the couple's lives.

Some may claim they cared for you as a child and now you are married and not caring for them. So instead of supporting you to build your family or relationship, they will rather cause discord or misunderstanding between you and your partner so that you can run back to them or tell them everything going on in your marriage.

Whatever be the case, you must learn to talk about such things as couples and deal with them together. Never think you can deal with family members on your own especially when the agenda of these individuals are not really known.

Although we have some lovely and great supportive family members who want the best for us, sometimes, it can be very difficult when we have those who are not but would want to split our relationships. When this happens, we need to make the right decision for the preservation of our relationship with our partners.

Are you dealing with some family members who are ruining your relationship? Please, talk about it now with your partner before things get of hand.

Sadly, when things are not spoken about in the relationship regarding these negative family members, they cause high level of stress, anxiety and even depression to our partners especially during family gatherings.

Some of these family members can go to the extent of calling your partner names whenever he or she is around them. This can lead your partner to pretend to be happy around them although he or she is bruising and hurting painfully. It can even turn your partner into a two-faced person just because he or she does not want to be seen as a snob or troublesome person in the face of misunderstanding with any family member.

This will not help or encourage your partner to express him or herself fully among some of these family members who are constantly destroying his or her self-confidence, morale or even reduce his or her ability to function productively. You must be able to identify and avoid those family members whose plans and desires are to cause division between you and your partner. As couples, it is your responsibility to ensure that no family member comes to sow seeds of discord or division in your relationship.

You must both be vigilant and watchful over your marriage. The way you both treat your relationship is exactly how other family members will want to treat it. By now, you must know those who put pressure on your relationship and find way to deal with them or avoid them.

Avoiding negative family members is not a sin or evil. It is rather wicked when you know those who have the potential to cause trouble for your partner and you never gave them warning or took steps to inform your partner for him or her to be caught up in their evil moves.

Being around negative family members can drain your partner's energy and cause them to feel trapped and overwhelmed. Therefore, create enough time to talk to your partner about how he or she can avoid them and still apply wisdom to dwell with them sensibly to prevent them from feeling hurt and neglected by your partner.

If you discover that you are not able to get along with some family members of your spouse, it must be addressed. When you do this, it will help to keep things in the right perspective.

It is true that we are all created to deal with issues differently. Thus, dealing with such troublesome in-laws can be challenging especially if your partner or you are the shy type. Your partner may not be very open when discussing certain family issues and if that is the case, you must help your partner to overcome his or her fear by not talking about such things among some family members.

We must remember that every relationship is totally different and how we deal with issues that arise within the family need different approaches to handle them. Therefore, a couple dealing with family members on a particular issue is going to be different from how a friend of the couple will deal with theirs.

So if you and your spouse are feeling the negative impact of some family members on your relationship, you must talk about it. This can only be possible if you both allow effective communication to be part of the relationship.

Avoid speaking to each other about these family members when you know it will result into argument and misunderstanding. Never talk immediately when you hear negative things about your partner. It is very important to remain calm and relaxed until the individual is not around to interfere with your conversation.

Dealing with in-laws in your relationship can be very challenging. You must be smart and wise like a serpent and harmless like a dove in order to dwell with in-laws.

Never get into an argument with any of your in-laws; speak to your partner about any issue you have about them. Try to avoid a fight with them as they can turn the fight on you. Whatever it is, you must stand by your partner and do not try to paint them bad in front of your parents or speak negatively about your in-laws to your partner. Remember that they are your partner's family members and anything said in the wrong way might cause a bigger challenge between you and your spouse.

If you discover that a family member has the potential to turn up in your relationship, you must both set a standard for him or her. Unfortunate, this could be very difficult among some African families. Telling them to call before visiting will break hell loose on you or your partner. Therefore, wisdom must be applied when handling such controversial family members so that they do not ruin your marriage.

Some family members can go the extent of not showing you respect, and love. Some would not even take their time to get to know you in person yet expect you to know and respect them. When this happens, it is your duty to speak to your partner to deal with them sensibly. Don't ever feel rejected. Not everyone will make your life a happy one in your marriage and knowing this will help you put yourself on guard and ignore every stone thrown at you.

It can be tempting to want to complain about your partner to his or her parents or family members but it must be done with care. Sometimes couples blame their spouses for the misbehaviour of some family members. This is not a healthy move to take. Avoid blaming your spouse for every single thing that happens as a result of his or her family members.

As mentioned earlier, not every family member will be happy with your relationship. Therefore, you must be ready to accept that some problems may arise from some of these people. You must learn to blend in but do not kill yourself for any of them as you are not married to them but your partner.

One of the biggest mistakes I have made in my marriage is to share my marital challenges with some family members I thought were there to support me and have the interest of our relationship at heart. It turned up that I was digging the grave for my marriage. Things got so bad that it affected the relationship my wife had with some of them. It was not the best thing I did. So, I have decided to deal with issues within the marital home to avoid writing the obituary of my marriage.

Sharing information about your relationship with some family members will create envy, jealousy, and hurt among these members which are not healthy for the growth of your relationship. Family members are very protective of their children. This means, you must be careful how you speak about your partner to their parents or family members before they attack you.

 I have learned that nobody wants to know or hear negative things about their relative. So you must avoid painting your partner black before your family or theirs. Whatever it is, you can both talk about it and resolve it amicably without telling the whole story to those who cannot be of help.

No matter how loving and peaceful you think your relationship is, some family members can ruin it within a second. Therefore if you value and want a lasting relationship, you must learn to communicate and share with your spouse without fear. Failing to deal with some in-laws can land your marriage in divorce.

No matter what, you and your partner have the obligation to protect your relationship against any negative and controlling family members. You must do everything possible to maintain your relationship regardless of extended family challenges.

The success of your relationship with your partner should be your number one focus. Never allow anyone from your family members to come and sow evil seeds in your relationship that may affect the marriage. Be real and frank with your family members or your partner's and let them see the love you have for each other. Do not show any crack in the relationship to them. When you do, you will only give them the licence to cause havoc in the marriage.

You were put together to build each other up, to encourage one another, and to have a great and strong family life. Be wise and never allow family members to destroy your home.

What therefore God has joined together, let not man put asunder.

Chapter Thirteen

DEAL WITH YOUR DIFFERENCES

What makes us all different in life are the individual beliefs and values we hold. These values and beliefs are the things we see as important to our lives because they have helped to shape us.

Most often, couples seem to share the same values and beliefs which help to bring understanding. However, where those values and beliefs are different, it is very important that couples find ways to discuss these differences in order to have a common ground to relate and live peaceably.

This is one of the reasons why effective communication is vital in building and forming formidable relationships among couples. Although communication is important in determining the longevity of any relationship, it only becomes effective when the conversation is based on the values and belief systems of the people involved. Knowing each other's values and beliefs help to dwell and live together happily in the relationship.

Never get into a relationship to change your partner

Changing the personality (values and beliefs) of your partner is not going to be easy. Don't get me wrong; some values and beliefs can be very useful for the relationship as it may help to keep the partner in check.

Therefore, it is very necessary to identify the values and beliefs your partner has to help you understand the way he or she thinks and behaves. When this is identified, couples are able to work things out together and accommodate their partner easily and reduce unnecessary stress in the marriage.

The challenging issue that faces couples is when the personality of a partner gets in the way of the other and causing misunderstandings in the relationship. A partner who is selfish and spends his or her money alone can bring problems. So differences in values and beliefs should be discussed before it creates conflicts for the relationship.

I am not advocating that couples should have the same values and belief systems. However, it will be advisable to have a common perspective for a successful relationship.

Couples who seem to have issues with each other's values and beliefs should talk about them in-depth. This helps to respect each other as human beings with unique interests and appreciate differences. No couple is ever the same. They are different with special values and beliefs. These values and beliefs are the things that set them apart from other couples. Our authenticity is in our values and beliefs. They are the things that make us happy and have good life as they are based on our learning experiences. We may have observed them or acquired them from our natural parents.

> **"Do not be bound together with unbelievers; for what partnership has righteousness and lawlessness, or what fellowship has light with darkness?"**
>
> **2 CORINTHIANS 6:14**

From the Scripture, it is very clear as to why it is not advisable to live or have a relationship with someone you do not have common values and beliefs. Having a great communication as couples can help avoid the challenges that may arise as a result of difference in values and beliefs. This is because, you will have the time to speak and talk about those differences amicably and resolve any conflicts associated with them.

It is never too late to talk about your differences as couples if you are ready to talk about and learn from them to solidify the relationship. However, no one is to be forced to go against their values and beliefs for the sake of the relationship. They can, however, choose to compromise in order to have a happy home.

My wife and I have differences in terms of values but have similar spiritual beliefs which have kept us together till date. We have learnt to ignore or compromise on some unnecessary things we hold dear which create issues and conflicts.

We have to agree to disagree on a few values and live in peace rather than pulling down the whole house because of differences in our beliefs. My wife is introvert. She has always been like that before we got married. It will be unwise for me to start fighting her to become extrovert within our short years of marriage. We both have discovered each other's personality traits and gradually learning to adopt and cope with our differences. This has helped us make decisions for our marriage especially when it comes to financial management, child care, and other family commitments without having to compromise on our individual values and beliefs.

We have accepted that regardless of our individual moral values, we can still work together to achieve a successful marriage; bearing in mind that every relationship has its own hurdle to face.

Recognise that you are not the same and can never be but can learn to embrace each other's differences and work to have a happy marriage. You do not have to change your partner to love them but love them just as they are and help them become what they are actually meant to be.

This can be possible only if each couple knows their respective values and morals through self-discovery. Couples who fail to understand their differences will have disagreements, but they should not allow their disagreements to prevent them from learning from each other's personality traits. Over the years, we have come to the conclusion that there are some unnecessary fights that we don't need to have in the marriage because they are not good for our health!

No one is perfect. As such, couples should learn to accept each other's differences and learn to forgive and accommodate. If you and your partner are finding it difficult to come to terms with your differences, then you both need to talk about things properly.

Sometimes, the challenges can be difficult to talk about but each of you must learn to respect each other and give room for listening. Listening to each other can help to create room for understanding. Yes; it is possible to be angry over some things but when time and space are created for proper discussion, difficult problems can melt away with simple talks.

Couples should learn never to shout or yell at each other during the period of discussion without a partner feeling attacked or suppressed.

You will be surprised to know that some relationships become complicated when partners are not sure about each other's values, beliefs, and the moral that govern their judgment and decision-making process.

Moral differences can be very interesting and stimulating for couples who are ready and prepared to learn from each other. Couples should embrace the differences each one brings into the relationship and see how best they can use that to build themselves up. No one is born useless. There is something great within each partner but when both fail to understand this fact, it will create a big gulf between the couples.

In view of this, it is advisable that couples learn to focus on similarities they both have and to work toward learning other traits of their partners that are yet to be discovered. Couples should not get into the habit of trying to change their partner but must learn to appreciate and embrace each other's uniqueness.

Most often, couples who think they can change their partners get into more trouble. They cause more harm than good. Regardless of the differences in beliefs, couples should not allow it to divert the main purpose of their relationship.

Talking about your beliefs as couples helps to understand each other and prepare and plan for areas of incompatibility which is possible through self-discovery. A partner who fails to discover him or herself will find it difficult to discover their partner's worth. Each partner must be real to themselves and in tune with what they love and like to do as an individual.

It is very sad how many couples spend time discovering their partners but fail to discover themselves and their own interests, needs, desires, future plans, goals, values, and preferences. The question is; how can you discover the differences in your partner and can't identify your own personal beliefs?

You can never give or help someone when you are in need of the same need. This is why self-discovery is vital in knowing who you are as a person in order to help your partner. Every relationship aims to succeed, but not fail. However, when couples fail to discover their own worth in life and in the relationship, it will be very difficult to express genuine love for their partner.

Couples should make time to talk and express how they feel about each other's differences. This can be in the form of sharing thoughts, feelings, opinions, values, needs, frustrations, and joys with each other. Under no circumstance should a partner feel not respected or value due to the beliefs and morals they hold.

Everyone is very important in the relationship and should be allowed to contribute and share things in honesty and must not be pushed to hide their true personality. Our personal beliefs and values are what make us who we are and what we expect to be in life. Therefore, couples should be aware of these values of their partners and try to work around them to have a great marriage. My wife and I have understood these principles now and working together to embrace each other's values and beliefs in order to have a successful relationship with each other and the children.

Do not take your partner for granted but value each other

Sometimes, some partners see themselves as "Mr Perfect or Mrs. Perfect" which tends to cause a whole lot of issues for them. Each partner is very important in the relationship and no one is superior or inferior to the other. So in any case of challenge, both partners should not be proud to compromise.

The worst thing that can happen to someone is to be seen as worthless in the eyes of their partner

As couples, we must not ignore the beliefs, values, and morals we have respectively. Therefore, talking about it and finding a middle ground to operate will go a long way to strengthen the relationship.

If you are worried and overly concerned about some of the values and beliefs your partner has, it is very important to talk about them peacefully. Most relationships hit the rack bottom not because there is no love but because each partner is afraid to talk about issues that affect them individually.

No one is allowed to die in silence. The only way to survive and not die in silence is to be able to speak about things that affect you and your partner. If your partner values and respects your view, he or she will listen and adjust to help you overcome your worry.

Never come to the point where you will be afraid to talk because you don't know how your partner may react about the discussion. Please note this: What you both fail to talk about in your relationship will surely find its way out into the public arena which may be more damaging to your relationship. So, talk about your beliefs and values amicably without intimidation or fear.

When we fail to talk about them, it creates room for disrespect, abuse, and taking each other for granted. These are some common reasons why most relationships do not last long.

You can't disrespect your partner and expect him or her to respect you

To respect and value each other's beliefs and moral values help to establish healthy boundaries within the relationship. However, lack of it may open doors for infidelity as a couple may feel undervalued, disrespected and not important. This could make the husband or wife to step outside to seek for attention and respect from an opposite sex leading him or her to cheat or engage in sexual activities outside the marriage.

As couples, we have the duty to talk about everything that disturbs us. We must and should be ready and willing to make positive changes to improve our relationship. When we spend quality time talking about things with our spouse, then we will build trust and honesty between ourselves and share things freely.

Every married couple wants to be accepted, respected, admired, and appreciated for whom they are and what they believe.

Therefore, when we fail to create the environment for that, we allow emotional breakdown to set in to hurt the relationship. One becomes very upset and angry because of these little foxes that can affect and limit effective communication between couples.

When this happens, most couples opt to live a separate life which also corrodes the relationship and destroys it. So, it is wise to learn to respect each other's moral values and beliefs about how they want things to be done. Also, come to terms with your spouse to work as a team to rebuild, revive and strengthen the foundation of the relationship.

Nothing is worst like living with someone you can't work together with

Partners should be ready to work in harmony to achieve the success of the relationship. They should never do things to hurt each other's feelings. Everything must be done in love and trust. "Greater love hath no man than this: a man lay down his life (values and beliefs) for his friends (partner)" (John 15:13).

As couples, it should be our desire and focus to treat each other with utmost respect. This goes a long way to boost the morale of our partners and enhance their self-esteem. Talk about your values and beliefs and never allow them to ruin your relationship.

Chapter Fourteen

PLAN YOUR FUTURE TOGETHER

Plan for the future by talking about it from today

Every relationship is built with the future in mind. You can never start anything in life without knowing or planning about how you can manage it in the future. Most of us desire successful and lasting relationships but fail to talk about it together.

Marrying today does not guarantee its success tomorrow if we fail to talk about how and what to do to ensure that the marriage with our spouse has a lasting plan.

The whole process of getting married is to move forward in life, and building yourselves a better future. But the question is; how do we start planning such a future when we don't talk about it?

This is the reason why this book is written to help you and your partner to learn to talk about the future. Talking about the future will help both of you to plan as a couple regarding how you would like to spend the rest of your life together and as individuals.

You should be able to ask your partner where they see themselves in 20 years. This question will help open the mind of your partner concerning how they view your marriage or relationship. This can also help to deal with any underlying issues that could become a stumbling block to the success of the relationship.

A relationship that has no vision is a relationship that is destined to fail

Couples who create or have a defined vision of the relationship stay together. Therefore, it is very necessary that couples spend time to talk about their relationship. They should be able to book a holiday or a quiet place where they can talk without being interrupted and in the process of talking, they plan for a successful future together.

Couples talking and planning their future is very important that it should be done without any distractions or interruptions. Being in a quiet place as partners will help you focus and appreciate each other's contribution.

How much do we know the hope and aspirations of our partner? Do we know their dreams? How well do we know that we can fit into those dreams, aspirations and future?

Talking about your future plans as a couple is a great conversation to have only if you both want to succeed and enjoy your relationship. As couples, please understand that the success of our marriage depends on the choices we make to improve it by learning to talk about things and planning for them.

Sadly, some couples have failed to see the need for planning for their relationships or marriage. This has killed the passion they had for each other hence collapsing the relationship.

A relationship devoid of communication and planning will be bankrupted of love

It is possible to wonder about what couples are supposed to plan about since they are already happily married and living together. You see, life is full of surprises and sometimes these surprises can lead to separation, divorce or even death. But, talking and planning about the future as couples help to prepare for any unforeseen circumstances.

Couples should be able to plan towards buying a house, the number of children both would like to have, the dream vacation they want. Understanding each other's future goals, dreams, needs and expectations becomes a priority for the relationship. This helps partners to talk and plan for their children and retirement age.

Sometimes, not every partner gets into marriage to start having children. So couples should plan when they are ready for children. A partner who thinks of having children at a different time should be able to talk about that plan with their significant other. When it comes to child-bearing, it must not be left to one partner to decide. Couples should be ready to plan how many children they both need and care for with the resources available to the family.

These days, it is challenging to secure and maintain employment. Therefore, partners should be able to discuss the challenges that may arise. The question is; how will you cope if both of you lose your job? Being in a relationship as couples is to be able to work together as a team and share the burdens facing the relationship and overcome it. This can be useful in planning family holidays together or separately. Whichever way you both want it, you must learn to talk through things and come up with plans that will benefit your relationship.

Sometimes, planning family holidays can be difficult for couples with children in school and managing their work schedules. However, with wisdom, couples can always find a way out through proper communication. This can be an exciting time for couples who are able to talk and plan well regarding the places they would like to visit such as the beach, family gathering, old friends and possibly some relationships that enhance and solidify their marriage.

Nevertheless, some couples fail to talk and plan their holidays and get upset sometimes due to misunderstanding and disappointment with their chosen destination. This can be avoided with proper communication.

When partners or couples are able to tackle the missing links, they will be able to decide the destination of the holiday and what sort of environment they would like to be, either at the beach, peace and quiet, or action-packed entertainment.

Deborah and I did not have a lot of fun time together when we got married because we were both active in ministry work. I could not plan for our honeymoon because of my commitment, dedication, and sacrifice to the man of God I was working with at the time. There was no chance for us to travel or go on holidays because the schedule of the ministry was packed.

As at the time, we did not recognise the importance of rest and family time because of the ministry work, but thank God for His revelation and an understanding wife who has helped me to create great holiday time for my family. As you read this book, I want you to know and understand that God values family time and rest. This change in my marriage did not just happen but we had to talk about it and plan in order to enjoy the peace my wife and I have in our relationship! To God be all the glory! Every day, we grow in grace. We are fully aware of the challenges facing our relationship as couples yet we are not going to allow them to prevent us from planning together to achieve the success we desire.

Another most crucial area couples need to plan for is children and the numbers they want. Raising a child or children is never easy as some have been made to believe. It takes and needs enough talking and planning to come to terms with when and how many children a couple needs.

Nothing prepares couples for parenthood unless talking and planning. However, I can appreciate that some children have been born into the world without couples talking and planning for them. But, as we get more informed, it is advisable that couples take time to talk and plan before becoming parents.

The fact that some couples in the past never talked or planned before having children does not necessarily mean you should repeat that pattern. Every relationship is very different and it needs a different approach.

Never limit communication to money, sex, infidelity, jealousy and cheating matters only. As couples, you must be able to speak about everything in your relationship. When couples are able to talk freely in their relationship, it helps them to do away with fear and live in harmony.

Talking and planning for the future must include when both of you are intending to have children, how you will both share the burden of childcare in combination with your daily work schedule.

The good thing about this is that it helps both couples to actually come out with ideas and plans that will work for the relationship and not put stress and pressure on them. Couples who communicate effectively can decide the work schedule for each partner in the family and how that can move the family forward! As individuals, we may have different public or private engagements that could be jeopardising the relationship and our commitment as parents. There is nothing wrong with having children just after marriage, but the most important thing is that you and your partner need time to talk about your respective concerns, priorities, and expectations thoroughly before children come in.

Talking about family planning with your partner is important in your relationship. One partner may prefer to have a large family and the other a small family. This also needs to be talked about so that there will be peace in the marriage.

No matter the reason you may have as couples, you must talk to your partner about childbirth and other health-related issues you may both have. Talking and having family planning discussion with your partner is very important regardless of how long you have been together.

Don't allow fear of losing your partner stop you from being honest about your fear and worries regarding the use of contraceptives. It is not a decision one can make alone, both couples must be ready to understand and support in such discussions. This will only help limit unwanted pregnancy in the marriage.

As in my work as a public health professional, it is important to encourage couples to talk and plan their birth control (contraception) methods together to prevent unnecessary stress and pressure on the family. Husband and wife should take the horn by the bull to talk and plan comfortably to arrive at a favourable decision as to what type of contraceptive method is suitable for them. This will go a long way to help share equal responsibilities in providing for the child(ren).

Although majority of pregnancies end in a normal birth, sometimes, things do not always go as planned. Sometimes, there could be underlying medical or health reasons why a partner may want to have one child or none at all. Whatever the case may be in your marriage, you must learn to talk and plan for everything before you are taken by surprise.

Chapter Fourteen

DEALING WITH CHEATING IN YOUR RELATIONSHIP

Cheating is like pouring acid on your relationship; it has the potential to kill the harmony you have with your partner. The question is: what is cheating and how does it manifest in your relationship?

Many of us may have an idea of what cheating means, but

> **"Let marriage be held in honour among all, and let the marriage bed be undefiled, for God will judge the sexually immoral and adulterous."**
>
> **HEBREWS 13:4**

how many of us know the effect of cheating on our marriages or relationships with our partners?

For the sake of this book, we can define cheating as a way of acting dishonestly against your partner to gain something from another person. Cheating can also be regarded as gaining or depriving someone from something through deceitful and unfair action without their knowledge.

Nobody wants to be cheated in their relationship. However, it is very important to understand why people cheat in their relationships or marriages and try to find solutions for it in order to rebuild your relationship.

There is no smoke without fire. Therefore, to be unfaithful means there is something that has pushed the partner to cheat. I am not supporting the idea to cheat, but to understand a condition, you must first identify the reason or root cause of why your partner is cheating. This is why it is very important to be clear with communication with your partner no matter how you feel. This helps to build trust and harmony within your marriage or relationship.

Partners should talk about infidelity in their relationships and try to understand how that could destroy and affect their lives when one engaged in it. Partners who have open communication within their relationship build boundaries around their relationship which prevents the creeping in of unnecessary hurts and cheating.

As I have mentioned earlier, every relationship is different. Therefore, we need to know that, there are different reasons why some people cheat in their relationships. So, if your partner is cheating or has cheated on you, then you both need to talk about it.

When partners fail to talk and communicate with each other to share true love and appreciation with each other, infidelity and cheating creep into the relationship.

Unresolved challenges can affect relationships and lead to infidelity. Couples should not sweep things under the carpets and pretend as if there is nothing wrong. What you fail to talk about in your relationship will surely find its way in the public and destroy your love life.

This book is written to encourage couples or partners to learn to speak, talk and deal with any underlying issues within their relationship to avoid cheating. Whether the unresolved issues originated from disappointments, misunderstandings or hurts, please, create room to talk about it with your partner to reach a satisfactory resolution.

As human beings, we love appreciation and affection from our fellow men. So, when you don't show and demonstrate respect and love to your partner, there is the tendency for them to seek it from another person outside the marriage.

Showing affection to our partners shows them how much we love them. They feel good and very important in the relationship. This motivates them to do everything possible to keep and maintain faithfulness no matter the challenges or temptation to cheat.

Partners have the responsibility to ensure that communication becomes the pillar of their relationship. This helps couples to determine what makes them and feel fulfilled without feeling ignored or neglected. Talking and sharing love moments such as cooking, walking, watching television, and listening to music together will bind your relationship and help it to withstand the storms of life.

If you are the partner who loves or responds to physical affection from others especially from the opposite sex or you are the one who gets turned off by physical affection in public, try and speak with your partner and come to agreement as to how to handle this sort of affection from your partner. When it is not ironed out between you and your partner, it can lead your partner to think he or she is not being loved.

Your love for your partner should be greater than their mistakes

We all make mistakes in life and mostly in our relationships. However, it takes genuine love for your partner to overlook and forgive your partner whenever they make mistakes.

When couples fail to forgive each other and understand their partner's limitations, they are more likely to be hurt. When a partner gets hurt and feels vulnerable, they can step outside to seek love and affection from the opposite sex who may be showing respect and appreciating them better than their partner at home. Hurt can lead to resentment and frustration from the part of your partner. This is the reason the love for your partner should be greater than their mistakes.

Holding on to mistakes or hurts can punch a heavy blow to your relationship and prevent you from resolving and moving on with your partner.

When a couple holds on to unforgiveness, hurts, and mistakes of their partner, the relationship gets destroyed. Therefore, such issues should be talked about and resolved quickly!

Partners should be ready to let go of resentment in the relationship and try to talk about anything that affects them. Sometimes, couples step out to cheat on their partner because of hurts. Couples should never allow their ego to push them to cheat or betray the trust, respect and value their partners have for them.

We must learn to pay attention to the little things that create hurts in the relationship with our partner and find ways and means to build trust with our partners.

Let us not forget that anyone can be hurt and that can lead anyone to seek comfort and affection. This means that both husband and wife have the tendency to cheat but it takes maturity and determination to remain faithful in the relationship. Partners who are not respected or feel less valued in the relationship may be tempted to cheat with the opposite sex who shows respect and appreciates them for whom they are.

With the increase of technology and access to social media, cheating has become more prevalent and acceptable in most relationships. This is because couples spend less time talking about issues that affect them but spend more time on social media chatting and cheating.

Yes, it is possible to argue that not everyone cheats on social media. However, when partners fail to talk to each other, they may have the temptation to share it with the opposite sex on the Internet which can lead to infidelity and cheating within the relationship.

It is important to suggest that whether one is cheating or not, couples should spend less time chatting with the opposite sex who are not married or have something to help build their relationships on social media.

Communication is the only bridge that leads to forgiveness

As a lifestyle coach, there were times and occasions I had to help couples through situations where affairs were birthed through social media. Cheating over the Internet or social media sites only become an option for the couples who do not create valuable time for their relationship and family.

If a partner gets involved emotionally or psychologically with a person over the Internet and begins to find attachment and belonging to this person, it becomes unhealthy for any marriage relationship.

Do not allow cheating to ruin or destroy your relationship. Sit together and talk about your differences and come out with solutions to them. Whatever the case affecting your communication in the relationship, please, talk about it maturely with your partner and never use social media to get away with murder. Cheating must not be allowed in healthy relationships as it has the ability to lead to relationship breakup and divorce.

No one puts hot food in his or her mouth and doesn't get burned

It does not matter how cool a partner thinks cheating is, it has the potential to burn your relationship down. Every effort must be made to avoid cases of infidelity occurring in your relationship. Cheating does not only affect your partner, but you the cheater.

Have you ever sat down and thought how one gets burned with fire and the consequences on the individual's health? Well, the same thing happens to anyone who thinks he or she is cheating on their partner. They are setting themselves on fire. What happens to the body when it is set on fire?

Cheating can cause an excruciating pain on your relationship and affect your ability to think sensibly. When couples cheat on their partners, they send the relationship into shock just as the body gets into shock of fire destroying the foundation and the fabric of the relationship. This is why it is not a good thing to avoid talking about things in your relationship.

Couples should understand that being in each other's life means they are there to provide emotional support and attachment. Neglecting this will consequently affect the relationship by pushing a partner to cheat outside the marriage.

A partner who is on the brink of having an affair should be very careful and seek for help by coming clean to talk about it. Be honest about your situation and never allow pride or fear to throw you into the habit of cheating because once you get into that behaviour, it may be very difficult to come out especially if you are the attention-seeking individual.

Communication creates honesty within a relationship

Like any addiction, cheating can be addictive and once you are caught up in its jaws, you will probably need a hammer to set yourself free. It is not a good thing to put a partner through such situations because it can also lead to health challenges like stress, worry, anxiety and hypertension.

Couples must do everything they can do to avoid pushing their partners into cheating at all cost by devoting time for communicating their needs to each other so that those needs can be met in the relationship.

When couples spend quality time with each other and share love moments together, it will be very difficult for one of them to cheat. This will however help to prevent the cheater from seeing other people!

Nothing hurt a relationship like cheating

Partners or couples should pay attention to the needs of their partner and try to understand what they yearn for from the opposite sex and see how best they can fill in those gaps.

Couples should not be reluctant or adamant to talk about infidelity in their relationship. They should not be afraid to confront the situation when the need arises. Talking about this fox will help to immunise the relationship against unfaithfulness.

Couples must learn to forgive each other in all ways. When you discover that you have been cheated upon, you must be ready to forgive quickly and talk about how both of you can move forward in rebuilding your relationship. Whatever led to the cheating must be identified and dealt with in love and forgiveness. Without love, it will be very difficult for anyone to think of forgiving a cheating partner. You can never remain a married person if you have no room in your heart for forgiveness. The marriage should be made up of two forgiving people!

Love and forgiveness conquer all things

As couples, we must understand that we are all humans and, to err is human but it does not give any partner the licence to go about cheating. However, knowing this will help us from being overly hurt by the offenses of our partners. There is no doubt in my mind that cheating can destroy any relationship, causing emotional pains and broken trust, dysfunctional family, low self-esteem and possibly severe depression.

Furthermore, it can affect the relationship the partner has with the children in the relationship, family members, work colleagues, and friends. In addition to all these woes, when caught in the act, it can create disappointment and embarrassment to both parents of the couples who may eventually ask for divorce. That notwithstanding, couples must learn to forgive their cheating partners before things get out of hand.

There is nothing forgiveness can't solve in a relationship

Cheating in a relationship must never be accepted to be a norm as it can have a devastating effect on the relationship most especially on the lives of the children in the family. No one should let the lack of communication make them cheat in their relationship. The communication lines should be kept opened. It is very important that each partner learns to appreciate and value their relationship and create an atmosphere of love, understanding, and prayers to avoid unfaithfulness in the relationship.

Couples should remember that when communication breaks, family, society and the world will fall apart. Therefore, each couple must work toward effective communication in their relationship or marriage to avoid it breaking apart.

Both partners must be ready to set or create an environment where they can share their emotions and concerns freely without fear. By so doing, each can forgive the other and take steps into rebuilding trust, love, and respect for the marriage.

Trust is like the fire that warms and strengthens our relationships

Trust plays an important role in strengthening the relationship with our partner. It helps to build security in the face of challenges. Therefore, when we allow cheating to creep into our relationship, that trust is broken and creates insecurity and fear.

It is not always easy to express trust when we have been cheated upon. Insecurities, fears and doubts become bigger than the trust we have for each other when cheating sets into the relationship, weakening and wrecking the very fabric of the love we have for each other.

Nothing is stronger than love and forgiveness. Talk about everything in your relationship, but don't forget to love and forgive. May you receive grace to rebuild what unfaithfulness has destroyed in your marriage!

Chapter Fifteen

DON'T FIGHT
OVER HOUSE CHORES

Talk About Them

Every relationship has its own challenges as we have identified throughout the various chapters in the book. We have discovered that, for us to have a great and successful relationship, we have to commit ourselves to effective communication as couples to share our values and beliefs together. This will help us to maintain and have long lasting relationship with our partners.

Most marriages or relationships are faced with their own challenges which include money, infidelity, insecurity or unfaithfulness. On the other hand, some relationships are faced with basic issues like how to handle household chores.

Household chores can become a serious challenge in relationships where both couples fail to communicate their need and share things amicably to create the atmosphere of love and understanding.

This becomes a challenge in most relationships because couples fail to communicate effectively on how they can share the household chores and to make sure it does not control their marriage. Communication as we have discovered is the means by which we express ourselves towards our partners. It takes effective communication to understand your partner and to relate with them on the level he or she wants.

Therefore, when it comes to how house chores are done and managed, couples must be able to communicate that need to their partner without being seen as a controller or nagger. Couples should be able to talk about house chores and see how best they can resolve the challenges associated with it so that their relationship doesn't suffer a breakdown.

It is therefore imperative that couples who see house chores as a major challenge to their relationship set aside time to talk and discuss about it before their marriage is destroyed.

Couples should be able to talk to each other regarding who does what in the relationship especially where one partner is seen to be doing everything in the house without any assistance from their partner. Under no circumstance should a partner feel less important or feel like a slave in a relationship, and couples should be able to ask for help from their partner to assist them to keep the house the way they both want it to be. Research has proven that couples who do household chores together have a lasting marriage.

My wife and I have come to discover the truth of sharing house chores without fighting each other. This has become the structure and the foundation on which we teach and educate our children. I have observed that over the years, we have felt resentful at each other especially when the household chores were not done or the house kept untidy until we decided to get to the bottom of it. It was lack of communication and respect for each other's values that made us resentful towards each other when the household chores were not done.

This therefore means that a couple should have a defined way of sharing household chores between themselves. They should be able to work together to keep their home the way they want for themselves and not how one person wants it.

Household chores can vary from relationship to relationship so it is very important that each couple looks at what sort of household chores they have without comparing their relationship with others in order to address their own challenges. This can be from organising objects, managing storage issues, meal preparation, cleaning, and outdoor work to childcare. For example, bathing, dressing, grooming, feeding, and putting the children to bed. My wife and I have managed very well in this area and we are still working at it every day.

Over the years, we have taken on increasing amounts of our children's school work and wellbeing. Even though things were very challenging for us especially with the nature of jobs we do as health workers, we have been able to communicate the need of our sharing the chores.

My wife takes care of shopping, meal preparation, vacuuming, toilet cleaning, etc. Whiles I take care of the bill payments and the children's academic work to ensure that none of us is overworking or seen as a slave. I take our son to football each Saturday. Sometimes, it is difficult yet I still try to take him after my night shift on Saturday morning before I come back to have some sleep. These would not have been possible if we had not spoken intensively about them as a couple and this has helped to reduce fight and resentment.

Nevertheless, sharing household chores can be difficult for some couples to do or manage, but with understanding and communication, it can be done in respect.

Communication takes away fight and resentment from a loving relationship especially when it comes to sharing of household responsibilities. In view of this, it is crucial that couples talk about their household chores and come to conclusion on how to share their burdens.

In a relationship, there is nothing like the best or right way. What matters the most is effective communication to move it to the next level. Couples who are or get frustrated with their household chores should do everything possible to talk over things respectfully without arguing over them. Arguing over chores in your relationship will only create division and gap in the relationship instead of mending the broken bridges. It doesn't mean you should not speak or express your concern about things in your relationship but don't let it become the reason for your fight or separation.

Just as my wife and I were ignorant about what to do to keep our relationship from petty fight due to household chores, it is worth saying that some couples out there can be going through the same thing. However, if couples can sit down and go back to the drawing board to set their priorities right, there is nothing they cannot do together in harmony and love.

Every couple should be able to talk about what matters to them and should never compare their relationship with others because nobody knows what the couple next door is dealing with.

Every couple should mind their own ship and not paddle other people's canoe

Every couple should learn to discuss how they feel about their own home and come up with measures as to how and when they dust, clean, mow the lawn, pay bills, go on holidays and have great time.

Partners should learn to create time to sit down together and make a list of the chores that need to be carried out in the house just as we do with our family budgets. Couples must be able to know what they love to do and focus on doing it. No one should be left to do everything in the relationship because that can create difficulties and challenges for the relationship and that is likely to cause separation or divorce. Talking is the best way forward in dealing with issues related to household chores. When couples learn to talk about everything in their relationship, it will also help them to come out with the list of items that need to be focused on and attention will be given to such issues for a positive change. Couples should refrain from nagging, complaining, and criticising each other for the way things are not managed in the relationship. Criticising each other will not help but destroy the relationship.

We should never forget that we are all wired and designed differently. Therefore, rather than nagging and yelling at each other because of home chores, we should try to accept, appreciate and value the differences in our spouses.

Couples who are patient with each other when it comes to the issue of household chores tend to live in harmony in their relationships. They become flexible and allow each other to carry their duties in the house within their time and space.

When couples become more flexible, they grow together to appreciate what needs changing in their relationship and work towards to achieve them.

It takes a lot of time and energy to build a healthy relationship. Therefore, couples need to be patient with each other in their own developmental stages. Nothing should be done or expected to be done in haste. To be able to dwell peaceably with your partner, you must respect and value the marriage relationship you have with your partner. You must bear in mind that, like anything else in life, marriage relationships need time to grow, mature and bear much fruits. No couple should allow their partner carry much burden within a short period. Household chores must not drive your relationship to the wall but whatever it is, both partners need to understand the growing pace each other has and help nurture that within each other in the relationship.

Stop complaining and compliment your partner for the hard work

Gratitude and appreciation are the essential parts in maintaining a healthy relationship which help to build a warmer, stronger and happier union between couples. This however means that instead of complaining and nagging about everything that has not been done, a couple can show love and appreciation to the little things that are done by their partner and try to encourage their partner to keep doing more.

Most relationships or marriages will be saved if they make communication the foundation on which they tackle or handle any challenges related to household chores. At the end, it helps to strengthen the relationship between couples and make life fulfilling and productive. May your relationships overcome the hurdles of household chores that can prevent your relationship from growing from strength to strength.

Enjoy your relationship and don't let your household chores ruin it. Just have fun cleaning the home and enjoy working together!

Chapter Sixteen

PITFALLS TO AVOID IN YOUR RELATIONSHIP

A pitfall is regarded as anything unpleasant, hazardous, or dangerous that has the ability to limit, hinder, prevent and stop someone from stepping into their next level. It can also be regarded as a concealed hole or snare that waits to trap an individual to endanger him or her. A pitfall can also be seen as a pothole in the road. Therefore, in view of this chapter, it is very important that all the necessary pitfalls (mistakes) are identified and avoided in order to enjoy the relationship couples have with their partners.

This means that couples have to take intentional actions to prevent themselves from falling into pitfalls that have the potential to destroy their relationship and have a successful union between themselves.

Sometimes, couples make some serious mistakes that can put pressure on their relationship and if actions are not taken to avoid or resolve them, they can lead to the breaking or separation of the relationship. Some couples overreact towards their partners following some minor mistakes and that can break down effective communication and trust. To avoid the pitfalls in a relationship, one needs to have the right information or wisdom in order to handle the situations at hand. This helps couples to maintain the right atmosphere and understanding in the marriage.

Pitfalls also create unnecessary worry and anxiety in most relationships preventing joy and happiness. Couples who talk and share are able to identify the hidden dangers to their relationship and take steps to remove pitfalls that can create misunderstanding in the relationship.

The purpose for every relationship is to help build each other up in unity to achieve a common goal. However, when partners fail to identify the pitfalls that could harm their marriage, it will limit the progress of their relationship.

Every relationship is faced with challenges and mistakes but their ability to identify these mistakes or pitfalls will help them overcome them and drive their relationship further into the directions they have set for themselves.

No relationship is perfect; however, when couples learn to be vigilant and watchful of these pitfalls or mistakes, they will be able to do everything possible to overcome these pitfalls and work toward a great relationship.

Six pitfalls to avoid in your relationships

1. Controlling Habit

One of the most common pitfalls or mistakes that destroys most relationships is a partner's desire to control the other. Some partners have controlling habits. They see their partner as a chance to express their controlling attitude especially when they want to have their selfish ways.

This happens in a relationship in which a partner has lost the sense of communication and love for their partner. This mistake must be identified and avoided before the relationship is destroyed. When this is identified, you must talk about it with your partner and explain how such behaviour is not healthy to the relationship.

2. Unrealistic Expectations

Unrealistic expectations from each other can be very dangerous and affect the longevity of the relationship. Your partner is not perfect and so are you. Therefore, to expect too much perfection from your partner will put pressure on his or her health and make them ill and discouraged in the relationship. As human beings, we are bound to make mistakes. So, we should expect our partners to make mistakes and learn from them. We should never hold our partner's neck when they make mistakes. On the contrary, we should be their encouragers and support them to overcome their shortfalls and get better alongside as we grow together in the relationship.

3. Trying To Change Your Partner

Trying to change your partner into whom you are or what you want will only backfire. Don't forget that each and every one of us is created to be unique. Being unique makes us function and give our best to the relationship. Nobody has the licence to change their partners.

When a partner tries to change their partner, it causes havoc to the relationship. Most often, partners who suffer from personality disorder and obsessed with controlling others are the ones who get into relationships to change their partners except themselves. Under no circumstance should anyone get into a relationship and want to change their partners.

When this happens in the relationship, it creates an avenue for resentment, anger, bitterness, blame, fights, neglect and abusive behaviours. It must be avoided at all cost. A partner who wants to experience a good relationship must learn to work to change themselves but not their partner.

It is better to change yourself than changing your partner. Change is nobody but you. Avoid this mistake of trying to change your partner if you want to see long life in your relationship.

4. Keeping Secrets From Your Partner

When effective communication is broken in the relationship, it opens room for secrets to be kept. Sometimes, this is done in fear. This could be the fear of how a partner will feel or the reaction to their partner's past secrets, secret sexual partners, health related issues or the relationship they had with the other opposite sex. All these can lead to a partner keeping secrets from their partner. This however shows why couples need to keep the communication door opened to allow each other to feel free to share any secret or burdens that have the potential to damage the relationship when later discovered.

Please, do not get it twisted. I am not saying that you go about sharing everything you see and hear to your partner. However, it is appropriate to tell your partner things that matter to your relationship and both of you coming to a common ground to deal with such secrets.

Couples are not allowed to keep their personal health issues secret from their partner. Some health issues can be life-threatening and your not sharing it with your partner will only make life very difficult and stressful to your health and destroy the joy of your relationship.

Whatever reasons a partner may have for keeping secrets, it must be avoided because when the truth comes out, it will only be like an acid destroying the foundation of the trust and honesty of the relationship. There is nothing too late to share with your partner. Be open- and clear-minded to share things with your partner before they hear or find out in the public domain.

Never get into the habit of hiding or keeping secrets from your partner. Your partner is not a lion to devour you when you speak the truth. This is your chance to change things in your relationship by talking about that secret.

5. Making Assumptions About Your Partner

Making the mistake of assuming things about your partner can cause unnecessary trouble and unhappiness in the relationship. Assumption is the breeding ground for an unhappy and unhealthy relationship. It will even jeopardise the success of the relationship. When a partner finds it easy to assume things about their partner, it will prevent them from seeing the good side of their partner and then fall into the habit of thinking for their partner.

The problem with making assumptions of your partner is that a partner lacks the right judgement of his or her partner's action and starts reading or thinking into every step the partner makes.

Couples should avoid making assumptions about each other and begin to ask the right questions about why a partner took the action or made a statement. No couple is created by God to be a mind-reader. Therefore, a partner who is not sure or happy about his or her partner's actions should talk to that partner to understand the right reason for the statement or action rather than assuming things about your partner that will only create unhappiness for your relationship.

6. Taking Your Partner For Granted

Every partner needs to be given the chance to feel valued, respected, and appreciated in a relationship. Taking your partner for granted does not show respect and value to him or her. Regardless of the background of your partner, never take them for granted. Taking your partner for granted only shows your disrespect to their personality. As couples, it is necessary to learn to show appreciation and reverence to our partners and to go a step further to show gratitude to their support and involvement in our life.

Every partner is a useful and great asset in their partner's life. So, instead of complaining and taking everything your partner does for granted, show love and appreciation towards them. Genuine love for a partner takes away the desire to undermine and undervalue his or her effort in the relationship. Never take anything your partner does for granted.

When we show respect and value for our partners, they build confidence and energy to do more for the relationship and help to take the relationship to the next level; and not stagnate or sabotage it.

> "Never fail to appreciate someone who cares for you. Just because they're always in your life to help in some way, never fail to give thanks or recognition. To value someone or something too lightly is a risk no one should take."
>
> **UNKNOWN**

121

CONCLUSION

Communication is the lifeblood of every relationship. When communication breaks, relationships crumble and die. This is the main reason why this book is written to encourage couples to do everything possible within their power to talk about anything that disturbs their partner's peace.

Lack of effective communication in any relationship causes unwanted challenges or problems to the individual in the relationship. Nothing solves problems in a relationship as effective communication between husband and wife. Partners are supposed to share with each other things that pose as a threat to their relationship. These issues could be financial, respect, trust, love or unfaithfulness.

Couples should never feel too big to talk to each other whenever these issues show their ugly heads. Effective communication between couples enables them to sort out their problems with ease and have fun as well. Couples who share through effective communication strengthen each other and take the relationship to the next level. No one can ever build a strong relationship with their partner if they lack the ability to communicate effectively in a relationship.

No matter how couples feel about themselves and against their partners, when they embark on the road of speaking and talking over things, it will help them to build trust for themselves.

A partner who recognises that he or she is experiencing challenges in speaking to their significant other should try and create an atmosphere or arrange a surprise event for their partner to feel easy to speak or discuss on the subject.

A partner should pay attention to little details and never take things for granted in their relationship. Being able to pay attention to details makes a relationship very enjoyable to live in.

As we discovered from this book, communication enhances true love and understanding. Therefore, both partners are required to work on their relationship to ensure that their relationship walls are fortified against outside forces such as negative people, jealousy, hurt, cheating, and insecurity. Love for each other is built when communication becomes the main focus for the partners.

Every partner has something to offer the relationship. Therefore, couples should embrace each other's differences and values so as to work together to avoid the pitfalls that have the potential to destroy the relationship.

When couples identify, discover and appreciate each other's strengths and weaknesses, they are able to inspire, encourage, motivate, and empower with the necessary knowledge to grow and improve together. "Let's Talk About It Baby" is written to do just that.

It is therefore my fervent prayer and wish as you read this book and other books on relationships, you will be able to nurture and cultivate your relationship the way you both want it. There is no beautiful relationship anywhere except the one you both work together to enjoy. You are in this together. Talk about everything and never allow anything to suffocate your relationship.

RELATIONSHIP QUOTES

1. Genuine and true love is not just taken but given.

2. There is no need trying to convince anyone to love you. Love can be seen and embraced. So, stop chasing love's shadow of men and begin to love, appreciate and value yourself.

3. Live your life to please your maker. Never allow anyone to change you. You are not a television channel. You are more valuable than that.

4. Selfish people only make demands, but selfless people give without demanding anything.

5. There's one sad truth in life I've found while journeying east and west – The only folks we really wound are those we love the best. We flatter those we scarcely know; we please the fleeting guest, and deal full many a thoughtless blow to those who love us best. **Ella Wheeler Wilcox**

6. Shared joy is a double joy; shared sorrow is half a sorrow. **Swedish Proverb**

7. To grow in our ability to love ourselves, we need to receive love as well. **John Gra**

8. When men and women are able to respect and accept their differences, then love has a chance to blossom. **John Gray**

9. Man is a knot into which relationships are tied **Antoine de Saint-Exupery**

10. Relationships give us a reason to live. **Ronny Shakes**

11. Lust is easy. Love is hard. Like is most important. **Carl Reiner**

12. Let us be grateful to people who make us happy; they are the charming gardeners who make our souls blossom. **Marcel Proust**

13. You cannot be lonely if you like the person you're alone with. **Wayne W. Dyer**

14. Trust is the glue of life. It's the most essential ingredient in effective communication. It's the foundational principle that holds all relationships. **Stephen R. Covey**

15. Saying I love you is important, but not enough. Remember, love is a verb, an action word. Sometimes, passive because it happens to us, but also active, because we choose to do it. **Unknown**

16. Communication is the solvent of all problems; therefore communication skills are the foundation for personal development. **Peter Shepherd**

17. A good listener is not only popular everywhere, but after a while he knows something. **Wilson Mizner**

18. Nothing lowers the level of conversation more than raising the voice. **Stanley Horowitz**

19. What greater thing is there for two human souls than to feel that they are joined...to strengthen each other...

to be at one with each other in silent unspeakable memories. **George Eliot**

20. Love is like the truth, sometimes it prevails, and sometimes it hurts. **Victor M. Garcia Jr.**

21. Love can make a summer fly, or a night seem like a lifetime. **Andrew Lloyd Webber**

22. Everything that irritates us about others can lead us to an understanding of ourselves. **Carl Jung**

23. When you like someone, you like them in spite of their faults. When you love someone, you love them with their faults. **Elizabeth Cameron**

24. If you love somebody, let them go for if they return, they were always yours. And if they don't, they never were. **Kahlil Gibran**

25. Friendship with one's self is all important, because without it one cannot be friends with anyone else in the world. **Eleanor Roosevelt**

26. Forgiveness is the attribute of the strong. **Mahatma Gandhi**

27. Wise men speak because they have something to say; fools because they have to say something. **Plato**

28. The people who matter will recognise who you are. **Alan Cohen**

29. If you want to go quickly, go alone. If you want to go far, go together. **African proverb**

30. With the gift of listening comes the gift of healing. **Catherine de Hueck**

31. Love is touching souls. **Joni Mitchell**

32. A friend is one that knows you as you are, understands where you have been, accepts what you have become, and still, gently allows you to grow. **William Shakespeare**

33. Criticism is something we can avoid easily – by saying nothing, doing nothing, and being nothing. **Aristotle**

34. We would not have to forgive people if we didn't judge them in the first place. **Barry Neil Kaufman**

35. Make new friends, but keep the old. One is silver, the other gold. **UNKNOWN**

36. To avoid criticism, do nothing, say nothing, be nothing. **Elbert Hubbard**

37. When someone's character seems impossible to fathom, observe his friends. **Japanese proverb**

38. A true friend is someone who understands your past, believes in your future and accepts you today, just the way you are. **UNKNOWN**

39. The consciousness of loving and being loved brings a warmth and richness to life that nothing else can bring. **Oscar Wilde**

40. If someone does not smile at you, be generous and offer your own smile. Nobody needs a smile more than the one that cannot smile to others. **Dalai Lama**

ABOUT THE AUTHOR

Ferdinard Senyo Lawson is a Creativity Award (CA-AWARD, 2015) Best Life Coach & Best Public Speaker Winner, True African Heritage Awards (BEST AUTHOR, 2015) and BEFFTA Award Winner. He is the founder and C.E.O of Ferdinard Lawson Empowerment & Inspirational Agency C.I.C (FLEiA. CIC) in UK, public health professional, author, lifestyle coach, transformational and public speaker and publication consultant.

He holds a bachelor's degree in Public Health and Social Care and an influential member of Royal Society for Public Health (MRSPH) in United Kingdom. Ferdinard Senyo Lawson is married to his wife, Mrs. Deborah Zara Lawson, and they are blessed with two lovely children; Prince Joshua Seyram-Yaw Lawson and Princess Jessica Seynam Yawa Lawson.

OTHER BOOKS
—— WRITTEN BY THE AUTHOR ——

1. Igniting The Power Of Your Creative Mind

2. Your Backround Is Not The Ultimate:
    God Knows Your Future

3. No More Limits To Your Destiny

4. 152 Mind Supplements For Wealth Creation

5. 365 Inspirational And Wisdom Nuggets Vol.1

6. Immunising Against The Killer Bugs To Success

7. Success Within Reach: Re Conditing Your Paradigm

8. Faithfully Deployng The Spirit Of Servanthood

9. Bearing The Fruits Of Leadership

10. Let's Talk About It Baby Vol.1

www.ingramcontent.com/pod-product-compliance
Lightning Source LLC
Chambersburg PA
CBHW022135080426
42734CB00006B/377